BASIC FOIL FENCING

BASIC FOIL FENCING
Second Edition

by

Charles Simonian

The Ohio State University

**KENDALL/HUNT
PUBLISHING COMPANY**
Dubuque, Iowa

CONTENTS

Preface vii

Chapter 1   Introduction 1

2   Equipment for Fencing 7

3   Fencing Skills 11

4   Elementary Bouts 61

5   Rules and Officiating 67

6   A Brief History of Fencing 81

7   Class Organization and Teaching Ideas 85

Selected References 93

Index 95

PREFACE

This text has been written specifically for use in formal physical education classes in beginning and intermediate foil fencing. Its unique feature is its sequential presentation of the basic skills which any teacher can follow with some assurance that it represents a logical and orderly progression that has been tested over many years. Not every teacher will agree with the skill order, and those who do not should find it quite easy to assign reading by skill numbers in whatever sequence is preferred.

By having assigned readings for the class, an instructor would be free to spend full class periods on skill demonstration and practice. The need for verbal explanations of skills and rules would be minimal, and the students would have a study guide for written examinations.

Many excellent fencing books exist. The majority of these were written by fencing masters whose primary interest was the development of competitive fencers. As both a physical educator and a former university fencing coach, the author's interest in writing this book is to aid in the instructional process for students with recreational concerns out of which, it may be hoped, might grow competitive aspirations.

While fencing cannot be easily learned from a book alone, it should be clear that a beginner who lacks an instructor can more readily learn from a book which utilizes a sequential method than from one that groups skills without any indication of a progression to follow.

For those students fortunate enough to be enrolled in classes, it is strongly urged that assigned skills be studied before class so that the teacher's demonstrations will have more meaning and so that class time will not be wasted with needless questions.

Patient attention to the fundamentals will provide the base for unlimited enjoyment of this exciting and complex sport. The early formation of bad habits will place a limit on the student's progress, and correction of such habits is very difficult. Remember, practice makes perfect *only* if the practice is correct.

New teachers and coaches of the sport are urged to read Chapter 7 first because it covers many facets of methodology, class organization, teaching suggestions, and other related information of interest to inexperienced instructors.

Since the original printing of this book in 1976, a number of new rules and changes to rules have been adopted. Most of those which affect the beginning fencer are incorporated into this revision. Further, there have been several extensive changes to clarify the text, and photographs taken by David R. Matthews have replaced some drawn figures. Thanks are extended to fencers Michael Rodgers and Michael Faris who posed for the photographs.

chapter 1
Introduction

When fencing outlived its usefulness as a means of combat, it survived as a sport because it has always been an immensely satisfying form of physical and mental exercise. But fencing is a participant sport rather than a spectator sport, and it has never caught the fancy of the sportswriters or general public. One reason may be that the action is often too fast for the average spectator to follow, and some of the rules which govern foil fencing are not easily understood.

Is there any reason to learn a sport as archaic as fencing? While fencing is indeed an ancient activity, the word archaic certainly cannot be applied to a sport that leads all others in technology. As early as 1936, apparatus for the electrical registration of touches was used in world competition. Today two of the three fencing weapons are scored electronically, and the equipment is being continually improved.

There is only the most remote resemblance between modern competitive fencing and the old dueling styles, but fencing is still combat. The difference is that the lighter blades in use now have brought about lightning-fast action which demands a high level of athletic ability. The element of danger and the need for brute strength went out with armor and sharp swords, and what remains is the exhileration of battle, the physical pleasures of movement, and the mental challenges of tactical play. Put to the full test are a competitor's attributes of courage, skill, speed, agility, and cunning. There are few sports in which the action is so fast, where advantages are reversed instantly, and where there is so little time to make decisions or to act.

But on the recreational level, there is plenty of room for the casual fencer who wants only a bit of fun and a good workout. Most beginners, even those who are well-conditioned athletes, express great surprise at the physical requirements of fencing and quickly develop a respect for its value as exercise. Here is a sport that can be started as early as age ten and practiced well into middle age. Women find it to be a most acceptable form of combat sport which provides for every level of aspiration from simple recreation and exercise through the intense competition of the Olympics.

And fencing offers plain fun—what better reason for learning a sport? Enjoyment really starts when the beginner has achieved some control of his blade and body and is then able to match wits with an opponent. He is no longer merely hacking away, steel against steel, but can maneuver, set traps, fake, and finally be rewarded with the pleasure one feels when his blade bends upon his partner's chest.

Fencing does take time to learn well, and it is different enough that even those who have taken part in many sports will find that very little transfers to fencing. The beginner has to learn a new way to stand and move and has to discipline himself to resist the instinctive tendency to wield his foil as if it were a battle-ax. Unused muscles ache in protest at being put to such strenuous work. The mask and jacket are unfamiliar at first. But in time the student gets in shape for fencing, his movements become smoother, his flexibility improves, and he begins to look forward to the special pleasure that comes from having a good workout.

In the United States, a great many colleges and universities offer fencing in both physical education and athletic programs for men and women. There has been a rapid rise in high school interscholastic fencing with the result that many more experienced fencers are entering the college and amateur ranks than ever before. The recent development of age group and Junior Olympic programs is providing a broad base of new young talent which should result in an improved showing in world competitions.

Fencing is also found in programs offered by such private agencies as the Y.M.C.A., Y.W.C.A., Jewish Community Centers, and by community recreation centers. The biggest obstacle to the further development of fencing lies in the small number of available teachers. As in the past, our teaching needs have been met largely by foreign masters (maitre d'armes). American teachers have come from the competitive ranks with many teaching part-time as amateurs. Many coaches, amateur and professional, are members of the United States Fencing Coaches Association.

Competitive Fencing

Amateur fencing in the United States had been governed by the Amateur Fencers League of America (A.F.L.A.) until 1981 when its name was changed to the United States Fencing Association (U.S.F.A.). The U.S.F.A. rules conform to the international rules of the Federation Internationale d'Escrime (F.I.E.). Any serious student of the sport should have a copy of the current U.S.F.A. rules book and should be a member of the U.S.F.A. Amateur fencers are considered to be unclassified if they have never won a novice level meet. Classified fencers are rated as A, B, or C depending on how they have fared in important meets. An A fencer achieves this highest rating by having been a national finalist or by having won a major meet.

Many high schools, colleges, and universities include varsity fencing teams in their athletic programs, and the National Collegiate Athletic Association conducts separate national championships for men and women.

International Meets

There are a variety of international competitions and the more important of these are:

The Olympic Games (held every four years).

The World Championships (held annually).

The Pan-American Games (held the year prior to the Olympics).

The World Junior Championships (held annually for fencers under 20 years of age).

Competitive Weapons

Three different weapons are used in fencing—the foil, the epee, and the sabre. The weapons differ in construction, in certain rules, and in the target area involved.

The sabre is primarily a cutting weapon, although the point may also be used. The competitive sabre evolved from the cavalry sword, and its target area is from the hips up representing the most vulnerable body parts "above the saddle." Because of the wider movements and greater mobility, sabre is the most spectacular of the weapons.

The epee is a thrusting weapon which descended from the dueling sword, so it is logical that the entire body is valid target area. In concept at least, the epee is the simplest and has the fewest rules. Its bell is large to protect the hand, and its blade is the stiffest of the three weapons. In competition, epee touches are registered electrically. The blade has a push button on its tip and two wires are laid in a groove along the blade. The wires are continued by means of a body cord worn by the fencer and then through wires in a reel attached to the scoring apparatus.

The foil is also a thrusting weapon and has the smallest target of any weapon. Only the torso is valid target and, in front, it extends from the top of the collar down to the creases formed between the thigh and the lower abdomen. In back, the foil target extends from the top of the collar down to a line connecting the tops of the hip bones. Like the epee, the electrical foil is used in competition and is described in Chapter 5. In all weapons, five touches must be scored on an opponent to win a bout.

The foil is used by both men and women. By tradition as well as rule, the epee and sabre have been used by men only, but local competitions in these weapons for women have been sanctioned recently, and the first national championship in women's epee was held in 1981.

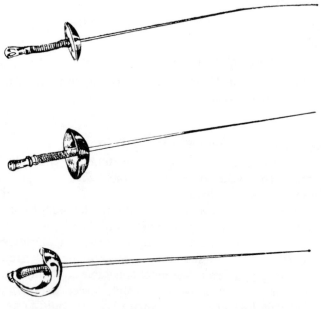

Figure 1. Top to bottom: French foil, epee, and sabre.

Emphasis on Foil for Class Instruction

Most instructors prefer to teach foil fencing to beginners for any of a number of reasons. One is that foil is the most practical and economical for group situations. Epees and sabres are costlier and more protective equipment is required because of the larger target areas. Also there is a greater hazard when a student is learning either of these weapons. A thrust with the stiff epee or a whipping cut with the sabre can cause some discomfort to a partner. These weapons are best learned in very small groups.

The foil offers the most in transferable skills, and once learned well, only a short time is needed to acquire the fundamentals of epee and sabre fencing. The basic stance, the footwork, and the lunge are nearly identical in all weapons, and there is some similarity in the defenses, attacks, tactics, and rules.

The training of a beginning fencer is normally along classic lines. As the student gains some skill and experience, he may begin to vary somewhat from the classic style and, by exploring positions best suited to his own build, to adopt tactics which reflect his personality and temperament. This possibility for the expression of self and for the development of one's own unique style is one of the attractions of the sport. The beginner must be cautioned not to experiment with styles until he has first learned the foundation skills. Sometimes, a student who experiences early success because of a particular attribute—being tall, left-handed, or quick—will continue to depend on his advantage rather than broaden his game. He must be told that his superiority will come to an end when his classmates develop the skills to deal with his narrow game.

Objectives of the Sport

As in boxing, the objective in fencing is to hit and to avoid being hit. However, in boxing strength is a major factor which is not the case in fencing where a fairly light touch counts as much as the hardest thrust. The rules permit any fencing style provided that the fencer does not use the unarmed hand and remains within the boundaries. Ducking and infighting are allowed, but physical contact between fencers is never tolerated. In addition to being touched by his opponent, a fencer may have a touch scored against him for such reasons as leaving the end of the fencing area, using his unarmed hand for defense, bumping his opponent, or violating certain other rules.

chapter 2
Equipment for Fencing

Whether your school provides equipment or you buy your own, you should know something about the various items and how to care for them.

Minimum needs for class instruction are the foil, the mask, and the half-jacket. Properly cared for and stored, this equipment will last many years. Fencing equipment supply companies will provide price lists and fully-descriptive catalogues that will outline sizes, materials, and ordering procedures. You may also purchase equipment from local coaches or through sporting goods stores.

Foils

The French foil has the handle most commonly used in beginning classes, and it is preferred both because it is considerably cheaper and because most instructors agree that it provides the student with a better feel of the blade. The grip covering may be leather, cord, rubber, or plastic. Some advanced students may wish to try other types of grips such as the pistol, the Spanish, the Italian, or any of a variety of cast aluminum "orthopedic" designs. When ordering foils, designate whether they are for right or left-handed fencers.

New blades are straight and need to have a slight downward curve worked into the first quarter nearest the tip. This is best done by holding the blade close to the floor and drawing it back and forth between the shoe and the floor. This combination of friction, heat, and leverage will also work in straightening blades which have developed kinks or sharp bends during bouts. The slight curve is necessary to absorb the shock of a touch and to help extend blade life by encouraging bending in one direction only.

The blunt foil point must always be covered with a rubber tip or with several layers of adhesive tape. These coverings do wear through and, while the point is not sharp, an exposed tip has the potential to scratch.

When blades are not going to be used for some time, a light coat of oil or grease and storage in a dry area will help prevent rusting. Rust may be removed with steel wool.

Replacement of a broken blade is accomplished by unscrewing the pommel, disassembling the parts, replacing the blade, and reassembling.

Masks

For class use, masks with plastic bibs allow for the easiest cleaning. If cloth bibs are selected, the snap-out type should be requested so that the bib may be laundered.

Masks come in small, medium, and large sizes. Since the manufacturers do not mark the masks permanently, it is helpful to stencil the size on the mask for the convenience of the students.

A storage rack can be easily constructed with wooden poles or piping mounted horizontally about two inches from a wall. With the headsprings slipped over the rack, many masks can be stored in a small space and equipment issue is simple.

A mask is most likely to be damaged when someone tries to adjust its size by pushing the headspring in and breaking the welded attachment wires. Headspring adjustment requires great care in bracing the mask before applying pressure.

Jackets

The canvas half-jacket has only one sleeve but provides the protection needed for beginning fencing. It has the valuable advantage of adjustable straps to allow wide ranges of fit. These jackets usually come in small, medium, large, and extra large sizes and can be ordered for right or left-handers. Women's half-jackets normally are slightly padded and have pockets on the inside to accommodate commercially available breast protectors. Since these jackets are fairly loose fitting, there is ample room to wear a sweat shirt underneath for added padding and protection.

The full jacket, which is mandatory for competition, affords maximum protection since it covers both arms and the entire target area.

Jackets are easily laundered but strong bleaches may weaken the fabric. Drip drying is suggested to avoid shrinkage.

Other Equipment

A regulation foil glove is desirable because there is a possibility of hand scratches caused by a partner's blade. The glove offers padding and is long enough to overlap the end of the jacket sleeve and thus prevent an opponent's blade from entering the sleeve. The major problem is that perspiration dries and cracks the leather, and it is necessary to apply some type of conditioner periodically. Gloves must be smoothed out and air dried to extend their useful life. Where budgets are limited, the students can provide any type of unlined glove as an alternative to the regulation glove.

Low-cut white tennis shoes are best for the average fencer, although light weight shoes designed for fencing are available. The beginning student should wear jeans or sweat pants for protection of the legs. Competitive fencers wear white canvas knickers and knee-length stockings, and of course, they also must have weapons and paraphernalia required for their events.

chapter 3
Fencing Skills

Skills 1 through 5 are basic body positions and movements which might be taught in the first class period. They will be repeated later in combination with the use of the foil. Instructors are referred to Chapter 7 for suggestions on course content.

All instruction is given for right-handed fencers, and left-handers must be alert to change the direction accordingly.

1. Attention

This is the position assumed by a fencer before saluting and taking the position of on-guard.

Execution

Place the hands on the hips. Standing erect, place the feet at right angles to each other, with the right foot pointed forward and with the right heel in front of and touching the left heel. Turn the body to the left so that the right shoulder is forward (Fig. 2).

Figure 2. Attention.

2. On-guard

This is the basic stance from which offensive and defensive movements are made.

Use

The position of on-guard allows a fencer to move forward or backward with equal ease and is the ideal position from which to launch an attack.

Execution

From the position of attention, with hands still on the hips, take a normal step forward with the right foot. Distribute the weight evenly on both feet, which are still at right angles. Turn the trunk to the left until the shoulders are aligned with the heels. Turn the head so that chin is parallel with the right shoulder. Bend at the knees into a semicrouch and keep each knee over its respective foot. Although the depth of the crouch is an individual matter, it should never be extreme (Fig. 3).

Common Faults

Placing more weight on one foot than on the other. Failing to keep the trunk erect. Bending the knees too much or too little. Spreading the feet apart too much or too little.

Figure 3. On-guard.

3. Advance

This is a movement toward the opponent in which a forward step is taken with each foot.

Use

A fencer uses the advance in order to get close enough to his opponent to be able to reach him with a lunge.

Execution

While in the position of on-guard, with hands on the hips, take a short step forward with the right foot; then take a step of equal length with the left foot so as to reassume the original spacing of the feet in the on-guard position. The length of the steps depends upon the distance that is to be covered, but it is preferable to take short steps so that balance can be maintained or the direction reversed if necessary. Movement should be rapid.

Common Faults

Initiating the advance with the left foot instead of with the right foot. Rising from the semicrouch of the on-guard position. Sliding or dragging the feet on the floor. Taking steps of unequal length with each foot.

4. Retreat

This is a movement away from the opponent in which a step is taken with each foot.

Use

A fencer can use the retreat to move out of reach of a direct lunge by his opponent or to maintain any desired distance.

Execution

While in the position of on-guard, with hands on the hips, take a short step backward with the left foot; then take a step of equal length with the right foot so as to reassume the original spacing of the feet in the on-guard position. The length of the steps depends upon the distance that the opponent closes toward you. It is preferable to take short steps so that balance can be maintained or the direction reversed if necessary. Movement should be rapid.

Common Faults

Initiating the retreat with the right foot instead of with the left foot. Rising from the semicrouch of the on-guard position. Sliding or dragging the feet on the floor. Taking steps of unequal length with each foot.

Drills

To practice the advance and retreat, pair off with another student and take the on-guard position facing one another. One person will lead and the other will follow as the leader advances and retreats as he wishes. The partner who is following must try to maintain distance during the drill and change direction at the same instant that the leader changes.

At first, this drill is performed slowly so that sudden changes of direction do not leave the following partner at a great disadvantage. Since this is a tiring exercise, the drills should not last longer than one minute at a time.

To the Instructor

An effective first drill in footwork is to have the class, formed in a single line, follow your lead as though you were an opponent. Take the on-guard stance facing the class. Give vocal commands to advance and retreat while also using a wave of the hand to indicate the direction and moving forward or backward yourself. After a few moments, stop using the voice signal but continue using the hand and your footwork as cues. Then drop the hand signal while the class follows your movement. Finally, put together two or more consecutive steps and make frequent, sudden changes of direction. Keep up a running commentary during this drill by calling out such cues as "point your right foot straight ahead," "take short steps," or "keep erect." To get across the important point that footwork is not mechanical, change the speed of your footwork occasionally and vary the length of your steps. The students must adjust their own footwork accordingly.

5. Lunge, Recovery from Lunge

The lunge is a long step forward with the right foot and is made by a fencer in an attempt to reach an opponent. The recovery from a lunge is a return to the original position of on-guard.

Use

The distance between two fencers is usually such that neither can reach the other without first moving forward in some manner. The lunge is one of the most effective means to move the fencer toward the opponent. The recovery permits a fencer to withdraw rapidly from a lunge to a defensive on-guard position, particularly after an unsuccessful attack.

Execution

To execute the lunge, raise the right foot, toes first, just clear of the floor and quickly but smoothly straighten the left leg. This action moves the body forward. At the completion of the lunge, the right lower leg should be perpendicular to the floor; the right foot should be still pointed forward; the left foot should remain where it was, flat on the floor and at right angles to the right foot; the left leg should be straight; the trunk should be erect; and the shoulders should be relaxed (Fig. 4).

To execute the recovery, push against the floor with the right foot and at the same time flex the left leg at the knee. Reassume the position of on-guard by replacing the right foot on the spot that it occupied before the lunge was made.

Common Faults

Leaning excessively, either forward or to the left, at the completion of the lunge. Failing to have the right lower leg perpendicular to the floor at the completion of the lunge. Allowing the left foot to roll during the lunge instead of keeping it flat on the floor. Failing to extend the left leg completely.

Rising to a standing position after the recovery and, consequently, having to take the on-guard position as a separate action. Dragging the right foot on the floor during the recovery. Leaning backward during the recovery instead of using only the legs to move the body to the on-guard position.

Note

The recovery can also be made forward instead of backward to the on-guard position. This type of recovery would be called for when the opponent retreats from your attack. In such a case, a rear recovery would result in further increasing the distance between the fencers, whereas a forward recovery would reduce the distance. The forward recovery is made by bringing the left foot forward to the on-guard position while the arms return to their positions exactly as they do in the backward recovery.

Figure 4. Lunge.

Safety

Foils will be used in all of the skills which follow. Rules for safety should be observed at all times. Some of the more common-sense rules are listed below.

Always wear a mask whenever practicing or fencing.

Never point a foil at someone who is not wearing a mask.

Be certain your foil tip is properly covered.

Do not use a foil which has a broken blade or a blade that is sharply kinked.

Wear suitable protective clothing. A sweat shirt is not a substitute for a fencing jacket. A torn or tattered fencing jacket is also unacceptable.

When carrying a foil, hold it by the middle of the blade with the point up and next to your arm.

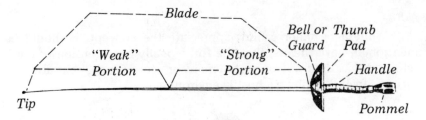

Figure 5. French foil.

6. Grip

Use

When the French foil is correctly held, the fingers can be effectively used to manipulate the foil. Too tight a grip will tire the hand and will hinder fine control of the foil point.

Execution

The thumb and forefinger of the right hand should oppose each other on the handle, with the thumb being on the top face of the handle no farther than a half-inch from the bell or guard. The other three fingers should rest lightly along the left side of the handle, which should be held against the palm of the hand (Fig. 6).

The French handle has curvature in two directions. The top surface of the handle has a slight upward curve and this surface is in the same plane as one of the two wide sides of the rectangular blade. The other curve is toward the right, i.e., toward the palm. When gripped correctly, the bend of the blade will be away from the thumb.

It might be helpful to point out that anytime a fencer is disarmed the bout stops immediately. Therefore, the beginner need not hold the foil so tightly that he cannot use his fingers to manipulate the blade.

Common Faults

Wrapping the last three fingers around the handle as one might grasp a hammer. Not keeping the foil in a straight line with the wrist and forearm. Bending the thumb at the first joint so that only the end of the thumb is in contact with the handle.

Note

　　While a beginner cannot appreciate the concept, it should be mentioned, nevertheless, that the foil is really an extension of one's self, and it is used not only to defend or score touches but also as a sort of "feeler" probing a hostile environment.

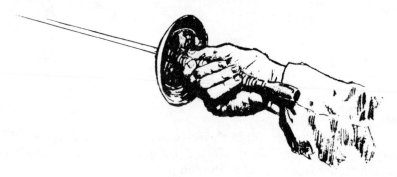

Figure 6. Grip.

7. Attention with Foil

Execution

　　Assume the attention position (Skill 1). Both arms should be straight and the hands should be several inches from the body. The foil is gripped in the right hand and is pointed toward the floor; the mask is held in the left hand.

8. Salute

　　This is a traditional gesture of courtesy that is made before the commencement of a bout.

Use

　　The salute is exchanged by two opponents before they put on their masks and begin to fence.

Execution

　　From the position of attention, the right arm—henceforth called the sword arm—is flexed at the elbow, and the guard of the foil is raised to face level. The palm of the sword hand is turned toward the face, and the foil is held vertically. The salute is then completed by smartly straightening the arm to a horizontal position (Figures 7 and 8). The mask is put on immediately following the salute.

Figure 7. Salute

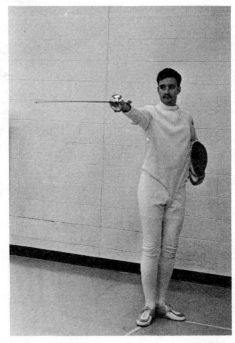

Figure 8. Completion of salute.

9. On-guard with Foil

This is the basic stance from which offensive and defensive movements are made.

Execution

From the position of attention, flex the sword arm at the elbow and raise the hand to a position slightly higher than the elbow but lower than the shoulder. The point of the foil should be at chin level, and the blade should form a straight line with the forearm. The hand position is such that the right thumb, as it is placed on the handle, is up and slightly to the right.

Raise the left arm and bend the elbow. The forearm should be vertical, the wrist should be relaxed, the fingers should be pointed forward, and the elbow should be at shoulder height.

After the arms are in their correct positions, place the legs in the correct on-guard stance (see Skill 2) by taking a short step forward and flexing at the knees.

Figure 9. On-guard with foil.

Common Faults

Placing more weight on one foot than on the other. Holding the foil tip higher than the head. Keeping the right elbow in contact with the body instead of several inches away. Allowing the left elbow to move out of position. Holding the sword hand as high as the shoulder or lower than the elbow.

Discussion

Since a great deal of footwork will be done while the student is on-guard, it is important that the stance puts no lateral strain on the knee joints. The knee should be directly over the foot. The rear knee is the one most likely to be strained as it is a common error to stand on-guard with that knee forward of the foot.

Anatomic differences will make it difficult for some students to assume the classic on-guard position, and the teacher need not force conformity. The principal objective should be for each fencer to find a stance which is both comfortable and functional. The best stance is one in which the least target is visible to the opponent, the weight is equally distributed onto both legs, and the sword arm is in a good position for offensive and defensive movements.

The rationale for the strange-feeling left arm position is that it helps to keep the left shoulder back and thereby reduce the exposed target. It also keeps the left arm out of the way of the action, and this is not unimportant when one understands that the rules forbid use of the unarmed hand for defense or for covering of valid target area. A warning is given when the fencer is judged to have used his left hand or arm for these purposes, and repetition during that bout will result in a touch against the fencer.

10. Advance with Foil

This is a movement toward the opponent in which a forward step is taken with each foot.

Use

A fencer uses the advance in order to get close enough to his opponent to be able to reach him with a lunge.

Execution

While in the full position of on-guard, take a short step forward with the right foot; then take a step of equal length with the left foot so as to reassume the original spacing of the feet in the on-guard position. The length and number of steps depends upon the distance that has to be covered, but it is preferable to take short steps so that balance can be maintained or the direction reversed if necessary. Movement should be rapid.

Common Faults

Initiating the advance with the left foot instead of with the right foot. Rising from the semicrouch of the on-guard position. Sliding or dragging the feet along the floor. Taking steps of unequal length with each foot. Changing the basic positions of the arms or of the foil.

11. Retreat with Foil

This is a movement away from the opponent in which a step is taken with each foot. It is the basic defense in fencing.

Use

A fencer can use the retreat to stay out of reach of an opponent's direct lunge or to maintain a desired distance.

Execution

While in the position of on-guard, take a short step backward with the left foot; then take a step of equal length with the right foot so as to reassume the original spacing of the feet in the on-guard position. The length and number of steps depends upon the distance that the opponent closes toward you, but it is preferable to take short steps so that balance can be maintained or the direction reversed if necessary. Movement should be rapid.

Common Faults

Initiating the retreat with the right foot instead of with the left foot. Rising from the semicrouch of the on-guard position. Sliding or dragging the feet along the floor. Taking steps of unequal length with each foot. Changing the basic positions of the arms or of the foil.

Drills

To practice the advance and retreat, pair off with another student, both wearing masks, and get on-guard facing one another. One person will lead and the other will follow. At first, the leader will move slowly one step at a time in either direction, and the partner will try to maintain the correct distance.

Gradually, the leader will take combinations of steps, will change his speed and his direction and even the length of his steps frequently, but he will be aware of the need to slow down if he is losing his partner.

12. Lunge with Foil; Recovery from Lunge

The lunge is a long step forward with the right foot and is made by a fencer in an attempt to reach an opponent with his foil. The recovery is a return to the position of on-guard.

Use

The distance between two fencers is usually such that neither can reach the other without first moving forward in some manner. The lunge is one of the most effective means to move the foil rapidly toward the opponent. The recovery permits a fencer to withdraw rapidly from a lunge to a defensive position, particularly after having made an unsuccessful attack.

Execution

The lunge is best learned in three distinct steps.

Step 1. Extend the sword arm smoothly so that the foil bell is at shoulder height and the tip of the foil is directed at the partner's chest.

Step 2. Lunge (as in Skill 5) by lifting the right foot, toes first, and forcefully straightening the left leg to move the whole body forward. Simultaneously, swing the left arm in an arc to the rear and downward until it is approximately parallel to the left thigh; the palm of the left hand should be up.

At the completion of the lunge, the right lower leg should be perpendicular to the floor; the right foot pointed forward; the left foot remains stationary and flat on the floor; the left leg is completely straight; the trunk is erect; both shoulders are at the same level; and the sword hand is still at shoulder height.

Step 3. Recover to the on-guard position by pushing against the floor with the right foot while flexing the left leg at the knee. Both arms are returned to their correct positions.

Common Faults

Failing to extend the sword arm completely before lunging. Lowering the sword hand during the lunge. Failing to extend the left leg completely. Rolling the left foot or lifting the left heel at the end of the lunge. Failing to recovery fully to the original on-guard position.

Drills

Practice your lunge before a full-length mirror and observe your form, balance, and crispness of execution. Pair off with a partner who will watch for errors and offer suggestions for improvement.

To the Instructor

With students in a single line, give vocal commands "one," "two," "three," or alternatively, "extend," "lunge," "recover." As the class improves, use only the command "lunge" but caution the students to continue to extend the sword arm distinctly ahead of the body movement. Finally, allow the students to lunge on their own, but advise them to remain in the lunge momentarily and check their own errors.

Discussion

The lunge is probably the most important single movement in fencing and must be learned very well. A great deal of emphasis must be placed on extending the arm just prior to the forward movement of the body, because most beginners will tend to move the body before extending the arm thus telegraphing the attack. During a bout, the official in charge (director) interprets a correct attack as one in which the arm is extended with the point continuously threatening the valid target of the opponent. It should be stressed that there ought not to be a pause between the extension of the arm and the forward motion of the body. The foil's progress from on-guard to the target should be an uninterrupted, fluid motion.

The length of a lunge will vary with the distance to the target. A lunge of maximum length is not always necessary, and, in fact, the early lunges of a beginner should be of medium length in order to avoid muscle or ligament injury. Most blade breakages are the result of a long lunge made against a near target.

Finally, the speed of the lunge is a direct result of the forceful extension of the left leg at the hip and knee. It should not be simply a stepping out with the right foot nor a "falling" forward type of action.

Although the direct lunge is the simplest of the offensive skills

Figure 10. Lunge with foil.

it is also the easiest to defend against. Excellent timing and speed are needed to score with a simple lunge during a bout.

When performing all of the following skills, the student must wear his mask. To don the mask, grasp the headstring with the left hand, place the chin on the chin pad, and pull the mask over the head. Since the right hand holds the foil, only the left hand is free for use in putting on the mask. To remove the mask, grasp the bib with the left hand and pull the mask forward and upward off the head. An alternate method of removing the mask is to reach back and grasp the headspring and then pull forward and downward off the head. Students wearing eyeglasses are cautioned to remove the mask slowly to avoid knocking their glasses off.

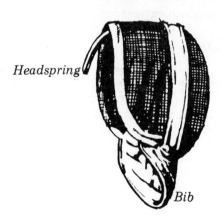

Headspring

Bib

Figure 11. Mask.

13. Hit

This is an extension or thrust of the sword arm which causes the foil point to strike the target without benefit of a lunge.

Use

The hit is a lead-up to the lunge. Through the use of the hit, the student becomes accustomed to touching and to being touched by his partner. The hit is also employed in making counterattacks (ripostes) which will be described in a later lesson.

Execution

Assume the on-guard position. The distance from the partner, or an inanimate target, should be such that a touch can be solidly made by extending the sword arm. Lower the point of the foil to the level of the target and then straighten the sword arm. As the point strikes the target, the blade should bend upward and slightly to the right. There should be no movement of the body or of the left arm.

Common Faults

Failing to make the two distinct movements of lowering the point and then extending the sword arm. Permitting the blade to bend downward on the touch. Turning the hand knuckles-up during the extension of the sword arm. Trying to touch from too slight or too great a distance. Using a punching type of thrust rather than a smooth extension.

Drills

Students pair off in two lines, salute, and put on masks. From an on-guard stance, Line A will thrust, Line B will serve as targets and as teachers. Either independently or on command, A will thrust, hit, and return on-guard; B makes necessary comments and corrections.

14. Lunge at Partner

This is the lunge with a foil at a person or target.

Use

The straight lunge is the simplest of the attacks and is the foundation for the advanced attacks.

Figure 12. Hit.

Execution

Until more skill is developed, measure the correct lunging distance by making a cautious trial lunge of medium length. Recover and make necessary adjustments in distance before making a second trial lunge. Then proceed to lunge as in Skill 12, using the three-step method. Upon striking the target, remain in the lunge position to make corrections in form and to see whether the blade has bent upward as described in the section on the hit.

Another method of measuring the correct lunging distance is to execute a hit from the on-guard position, and then, while maintaining this blade position on the target, slide the left foot backward until a full lunge position is reached. A recovery should be made and a trial lunge executed from this measured distance.

Common Faults

Failing to extend the sword arm before lunging. Permitting the blade to bend downward on the touch. Not aiming the point at the target during the extension of the arm. Making a longer or shorter lunge than the distance requires. Rolling the left foot or raising the heel.

Drills

As in Skill 13, the students will be paired in two lines. On command, the fencers in one line will lunge in three counts at their partners who will watch for errors in execution while also serving as targets. In the next drill, partners will work without command. Both will engage blades, that is, the blades will be in light contact. Partner B will give A a signal to lunge by moving his own blade a few inches to the right thereby opening his target. Upon seeing this opening, A will lunge and will remain in the lunge position long enough for B to make any necessary corrections or comments.

The final drill combines all the previously learned skills. Again from the double line formation, B will act as the leader and the "teacher" by advancing or retreating as he wishes. A will follow as in Skill 11. Periodically, B will stop, open his target, and observe A's lunge. Every so often, B will take one step back when A lunges to make A fall short, thereby providing valuable practice in the use of distance in defense and serving to remind the attacker that opponents do not always stand still to be easily reached. This, then, is the ultimate drill for these skills in that there is footwork combined with nonverbal cues to lunge. But it is a controlled drill because B will always act the role of a teacher.

Figure 13. Lunge at target.

15. Engagement

This is simply the crossing of blades by two fencers, neither of whom is attacking or defending.

Use

By contacting the opponent's blade, a fencer adds the sense of touch to the sense of sight as an aid in determining the relative position of his opponent's foil.

Execution

Facing your partner while on-guard, bring the midpoint of your blade into contact with the midpoint of his.

Note

Engagements are identified by number. When the opponent's blade is to the left of your blade and in contact with it, the engagement number is *four*; this may also be termed an *inside* engagement. When your opponent's blade is to the right of your blade and in contact with it, the engagement number is *six*; this is an *outside* engagement. There are other possible engagements, but four and six are the most important.

Four   Six

Figure 14. Engagement.

16. Change of Engagement

This is the act of making a change in blade position from one engagement to an opposite engagement, as from four to six or from six to four.

Use

A change of engagement may be made at any time in order to gain an advantageous position. It can be used when closing on an opponent who might attack as you step forward.

Execution

Lower your point, pass it under your opponent's blade, and complete the change by engaging the opponent's blade on the new side. Advanced fencers make such a change by manipulating their blades with only their fingers; however, a beginner will usually need to use the wrist, and this is acceptable so long as the forearm is not also used.

Common Faults

Failing to raise the point to face level at the completion of the change of engagement. Making the movement unnecessarily wide, probably because of forearm action. Striking the opponent's blade rather than simply contacting it.

Drills

Two partners will engage their blades but only the active partner will assume the on-guard position. The active partner changes engagements rhythmically and occasionally stops to call out the number of his engagement. The inactive partner observes and helps in identifying the engagement number or in correcting techniques.

17. Closing the Line

This is an engagement which carries the opponent's blade outside your body limits. That portion of your own target to the left of your blade is called the inside line, and the target to the right is called the outside line.

Use

By closing one line, a fencer is assured of protection in that line. For example, if you close your outside, or sixth line, you are protected on that side against the threat of a direct thrust. At the same time, the opponent's target will be open to a direct attack, since if your line is closed your opponent's line must necessarily be open.

Execution

With the blades engaged, move the sword hand horizontally left or right, carrying your partner's blade to the outside limits of your body. The wrist should be permitted to flex sufficiently to maintain the foil in the same relative position as when on guard. The hand is not rotated. The right elbow should scarcely move during the closing of the line. Now change the engagement and close the other line.

Common Faults

Lowering the foil point to below face level and thus having to move the opponent's blade with the weak portion of your blade instead of with the middle or stronger portion. Moving the sword hand across but failing to move your foil also—this results in the line's remaining open even though the hand is in the correct position. Moving the blade across without also moving the sword hand—again the line will remain open to attack.

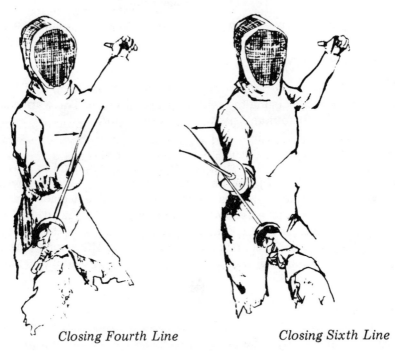

Closing Fourth Line   *Closing Sixth Line*

Figure 15. Closing the line.

Drills

The active partner alternately closes first one line and then the other. As one closing is completed, the next is begun by changing the engagement and then carrying the partner's blade horizontally across the opposite line. The inactive partner should not resist these changes but should offer a firm blade to be moved. The inactive partner plays the role of a teacher in watching for errors in technique.

Discussion

Where class time is short, Skills 15, 16, and 17 could be omitted entirely or only briefly demonstrated. In most bouts, fencers seldom engage blades except perhaps for an occasional instant. The terms should be understood, however, and the skills should at least be assigned for reading. Where time permits, drills in engagements, changes of engagement, and line closings are very useful in developing use of the fingers for blade manipulation. Drills can be with or without footwork.

18. Parry Number Four

This is a defensive action which deflects an attack made into the inside line.

Use

A parry is one of two principal methods of avoiding an attacking blade, the other being the retreat out of distance. There are eight simple parries, but four and six are the most important.

Execution

The movement is exactly the same as that involved in closing the fourth line (Fig. 15), the only difference being that the parry is used against an attack, whereas the closing of the line is made against a stationary blade. Move the sword hand and foil to the left just far enough to deflect the attacking blade away from your chest. As in closing the line, the hand must not be rotated. The strong part of your blade near your bell should meet the attacker's blade; otherwise the parry is likely to be weak.

Common Faults

Rolling the sword hand to a knuckles-up position in making the parry. Moving the sword hand to the correct position but not moving the foil point as well. Moving the foil point to the left but not moving the sword hand. Raising, lowering, or moving forward the sword hand during the parry. Parrying with excessive force rather than merely deflecting the attacking blade. Parrying wider than necessary, thereby leaving the opposite line vulnerable.

19. Parry Number Six

This is a defensive action that deflects an attack made into the outside line.

Use

A parry is one of two principal methods of avoiding an attacking blade, the other being the retreat out of distance. Parries six and four are the most important of the eight simple parries.

Execution

The movement is exactly the same as that involved in closing the sixth line (Fig. 15), the only difference being that the parry is used against an attack, whereas the closing of the line is made against a stationary blade. Move the sword hand and foil to the right just far enough to deflect the attacking blade past your right arm. As in closing the line, the hand must not be rotated. The strong part of your blade near your bell should meet the attacker's blade.

Common Faults

Rolling the sword hand to a knuckles-up position in making the parry. Moving the sword hand to the correct position but not moving the foil point as well. Moving the foil point to the right but not moving the sword hand. Raising, lowering, or moving forward the sword hand during the parry. Parrying with force rather than merely deflecting the attacking blade. Parrying wider than necessary, thereby leaving the opposite line vulnerable.

Drill for Parries Four and Six.

With both fencers being engaged, the defender signals his partner to lunge by opening his line—that is, by moving his blade away and exposing his target. The attacker extends and lunges on this cue, and as he does, the defender parries (closes his line). Both partners hold their positions until each has observed and corrected the form of the other. Occasionally, the defender should permit his partner to score so that the latter's part in the drill does not become dull and also to insure that the attacker is actually aiming at the defender. It often happens that the attacker anticipates the parry and unconsciously moves his point even before the parry is made. Occasionally, the defender may step back to cause the attack to fall short.

This drill may be combined with a footwork drill. The defender leads his partner in advances and retreats and then suddenly stops and opens his line to signal the lunge to begin. The attacker must follow fairly well so as to always be within lunging distance when the signal is given. Obviously, this drill must be strictly controlled so that the partner who follows is not placed at a great disadvantage.

Note

Parries have been described here singly, but two or more parries can be made in succession if the first parry fails to contact the attacking blade. Furthermore, a fencer may take a step back as he makes his parry so as to have more time to complete it.

Now that the parry and closed line engagement numbers have been discussed, it should be mentioned that when a fencer is standing on-guard without an engagement, his sword arm is said to be in a "position" whose number is the same as the equivalent closed engagement or parry. The most common on-guard position is that of sixth, which means that the fencer's sword arm and foil are where they would be at the completion of a parry six or of a closed engagement of sixth.

20. Direct Riposte from Parry Four

This is an offensive action by a fencer who has completed a successful parry four.

Use

By making a riposte, the defender has an opportunity to touch his opponent, who, being still in the lunge, is momentarily in a poor position to defend himself. The chance to score with a riposte is the primary reason why the defender will choose to parry rather than retreat.

Execution

Immediately after completing the parry four, lower your point and extend your sword arm in order to touch the attacker on the chest. The riposte action is the same as that for the hit (Skill 13); however, should the opponent be quick enough to recover to the on-guard position before the riposte can be made, the riposte can be delivered with a lunge.

Common Faults

Failing to lower the point and to aim before extending the sword arm for the riposte. Failing to complete the parry before beginning the riposte. Making the riposte with a punching or round-about movement instead of making a smooth extension and following the shortest path to the target. Holding the parry position too long before initiating the riposte. As will be seen later, the rules of fencing recognize the defender's right to riposte only if he does so immediately.

Drill

The defender signals for a lunge by opening his line (i.e., moving to the sixth position), and the partner responds with a lunge. The defender then parries and ripostes at the attacker who remains in the lunge position. After some skill is acquired, the attacking partner can parry the riposte and make a counter-riposte of his own from his lunge position.

21. Direct Riposte from Parry Six

This is an offensive action by a fencer who has completed a successful parry six.

Use

By making a riposte, the defender has an opportunity to touch his opponent, who, being still in the lunge, is momentarily in a poor position to defend himself. The chance to score with a riposte is the primary reason why the defender should parry rather than retreat.

Execution

Immediately after completing the parry six, lower your point and extend your sword arm in order to touch the attacker on the chest. The riposte action is the same as that for the hit (Skill 13); however, should the opponent be quick enough to recover to the on-guard position before the riposte can be made, the riposte can be delivered with a lunge. This riposte presents a problem not encountered in the parry-four riposte: the opponent's sword arm is usually in the path of a direct hit. The defender must then select the most available target, which is usually the opponent's right side just beneath his sword arm. The movement involved in this riposte is the same as that described above; only the point of aim is changed.

Common Faults

Failing to complete the parry before making the riposte. Lunging with the riposte while the opponent is still in his lunge and therefore quite close. Failing to lower the point and aim before extending the arm thus causing a flat or an off-target hit. Making the riposte with a punching or roundabout movement instead of with a smooth extension. Not taking the shortest path to the target. Holding a parry position too long before initiating the riposte. As will be seen later, the rules of fencing recognize the defender's right to riposte only if he does so immediately.

Note

There are two common defenses against a riposte. The attacker can recover very quickly from his lunge and thereby escape the riposte or he can remain in his lunge position and parry the riposte. The advantage of the latter defense is that there is an opportunity to score with a counterriposte because the distance between the two fencers is still close.

Discussion

While bouting can be delayed until more skills have been learned, at this particular point the students do have the basic offensive and defensive movements needed to fence an elementary bout. Short, controlled bouts can clarify the real uses for the skills being learned, and students will better appreciate the need for attention to detail in performing each action.

Since early bouts will be sloppy, it may be preferable, as a transition, to designate one line as attackers and the other as defenders and to consider these bouts to be "unstructured drills" in which winning is of no concern. It might be stressed also that all attacks must be directed to the chest area since the defenders have not learned to defend the portion of the target below their hand levels.

Before bouting can have meaning, the basics of the rule called "right of way" should be studied (Skill 22), and if very much fencing is to be permitted, it will be necessary to assign Chapters 4 and 5 at this time.

22. Right of Way

This is a rule rather than a skill, but it forms the basis for competitive foil and sabre fencing and must be understood by all fencers. The rule is derived from the logical behavior that might be expected of fencers using sharp-pointed weapons. The rule also provides a system for the awarding of a touch when two fencers hit each other simultaneously. It outlines a systematic order of movements and thereby facilitates the judging of a fencing bout.

Simplified Explanation

If sharp weapons were being used and a fencer were attacked, he would logically try to avoid being hit; he would not launch a counterattack of his own without first having assured his own safety. This is the basis for the rule called right of way. The fencer who first attacks ordinarily has the right of way and his opponent is obligated to defend himself by parrying or by retreating. The attack is defined as a threatening forward movement of the blade as a result of the sword arm being extended. If the defender succeeds in parrying the attack, he then can become the attacker by making an *immediate* riposte. With his attack having been parried, the original attacker must take the defensive before he can resume the offense. To gain the right of way, the defender need only deflect the attacking blade for an instant; it is not necessary that the parry be held until the attacker removes the threat.

A concept, which is not as important here as it will be later, is that of a threatening point-in-line. If the defender is standing on-guard with his arm extended and his point aimed at his opponent, the attacker who ignores this threat and lunges will probably cause both fencers to be touched. In such a case, the attacker is logically at fault because he should have removed this threat to his safety, usually with a beat action, before beginning his own attack.

23. Disengagement

This is an attack made into the line opposite that of the line of the engagement or expected simple parry.

Use

A direct attack is relatively easy to parry, and once it is clear that such an attack will not succeed, the offensive fencer can avoid the parry by passing his blade under it into the opposite line.

Execution

Assuming that your opponent is in the sixth position, extend your sword-arm as though you will be making a straight lunge. This feint should draw a simple parry four, and as it does, you must avoid that parry by lowering your point to pass it under the parry. Then raise your blade into the newly opened line and lunge at the same time.

Properly done, your foil will move continuously toward the target with no pauses between the feint and disengagement. It is the attacker's responsibility to avoid contact of blades which the bout director might interpret as a successful parry. The disengaging action should be done with minimal point travel.

Common Faults

Feinting unconvincingly as when the arm is not fully extended or the point is not threatening a specific target. Making the disengaging movement extremely wide. Delaying between the feint and disengagement, thus giving the defender time to parry a second time. Losing right of way by bending the elbow after the feint action.

Drill

Partners engage blades in fourth. As the defender opens his line to signal the start of the drill, the attacker should extend his arm to feint a direct attack. When the defender closes his line to parry, the attacker avoids the parry by disengaging his blade and then lunges. There should be no blade contact, and the touch should land on the upper chest by coming in *above* the defender's sword-arm.

It is important that neither partner waits for the other to do his part in the drill. Thus, when the attacker has made his feint extension, he should proceed to disengage and lunge because he *expects* the defender to parry at that time.

In a variation of the drill, the attacker is given the choice of making straight lunges or disengagements. The defender will react according to the threat that he perceives. If he believes the attack to be direct, he will parry four. If the feint is poorly made and he suspects that a disengagement is coming, he will remain in sixth which will cause the attack to fail. Finally, if the defender parries before realizing that the attack is by disengagement, he should try to reverse himself and parry six.

Discussion

Again, the drill can incorporate footwork as was done in Skill 19. It is most important that the leading partner pause before opening his line so that the following partner has a chance to get set. The leader can occasionally parry the disengagement attack and make a riposte.

The simple disengagement is an essential skill to master because beginners tend to avoid it or do it poorly and seem to prefer the one-two or the direct lunge. The initial feint must be made to resemble a direct lunge and thus cause the opponent to parry. The blade should move straight ahead just long enough to draw the parry but not long enough for blade contact to occur.

24. One-two

This is a compound attack involving two disengagements made in rapid succession. The first is a feint and the second is the real attempt to hit.

Use

When a disengaging attack has been successfully parried by an opponent, the attacker must realize that his opponent probably made two consecutive simple parries. Therefore, since one disengagement did not work, perhaps two disengagements will succeed in getting past the second parry.

Execution

Assuming that your partner is in the sixth position, feint a straight thrust to draw his first simple parry four. This parry should be deceived with a disengagement feinting into the newly opened outside line. If the opponent's defense was correctly predicted, he will now make another simple parry in an effort to contact the attacking blade. Now deceive this parry with your second disengagement and lunge immediately. From the first feint on, the sword arm should remain extended.

Ideally, the defender's parries should by anticipated so that both disengagements can be made *while lunging*; however, a beginner should learn this skill by remaining on-guard during the extension and first disengagement and lunging with the second disengagement.

Note that the name of this attack comes from the number of disengagements involved. If three disengagements were made, it would be called a *one-two-three*.

Common Faults

Failing to extend the sword arm fully during the feint and thus failing to convince the opponent that there is a threat. Holding the feint so long that the defender succeeds in parrying the feint. (It is the attacker's responsibility to avoid making contact with the defender's blade.) Executing the one-two by moving the foil with the entire sword arm instead of with only the fingers or the wrist. Bending the sword arm at the elbow between the first and second disengagements.

Note

The student must understand that the sole purpose of a feint is to cause the defender to parry and thus open up a line to an attack. If the feint does not resemble a real attack, the defender will not parry. A beginner often relies too much on the one-two because it brings his blade back to the larger inside line.

This attack is not intended to confuse the defender, but rather, it should lead the defender to believe that he knows where your blade is and that he can parry it. The tip of the blade should be quite close to the defender's bell when passing under it from one line to another.

Drills

To begin the drill, the partners engage in fourth.

	Attacker	*Defender*
Step 1.	Wait for cue.	Defender moves blade to his right to expose target and signal attacker to begin.
Step 2.	Feint a straight thrust.	See the threat and start the parry four.
Step 3.	Disengage feint.	Complete the parry four.
Step 4.	Disengage again and lunge.	Parry six, allow self to be touched.
Step 5.	Return to on-guard and reengage in fourth.	Return to on-guard and reengage in fourth.

As the partners learn to work together, the one-two can be practiced at bout speed by trying to start the lunge earlier, first as part of step 3 and then as part of step 2. Remember that increasing the speed of the drill does not change the manner of execution. Try to use only the fingers to manipulate the blade.

25. False Attack

This is any modification of a lunge that is made in order to give the opponent the impression that he is being attacked when in fact he is not.

Use

A false attack can accomplish any of several possible results. First, a convincing false attack will cause the opponent to react and reveal something of his defense. The attacker can study this reaction in order to prepare his real attack. Second, when false attacks are used intelligently during a bout, the opponent will be uncertain as to when the actual attack will be made, and he will be kept off balance. Finally, a false attack can be used to temporarily stop the advance of an aggressive opponent.

Execution

The most common false attack is a simple lunge that is deliberately short of the target. This short lunge may or may not be accompanied by a blade movement such as a disengagement, a one-two, or a beat. A false attack can also be made by simply stamping the right foot in place while making a threatening extension of the sword arm.

Common Faults

Making the false lunge too long and thus being in danger of being hit by the opponent. Making the movement unconvincingly and getting no reaction from the opponent.

Discussion

False lunges are useful at the beginning of a bout with a new opponent. When done effectively, they get reactions from the opponent, and these reactions must be noticed, analyzed, and "filed away" for possible later use in the bout.

A false lunge is often ignored by the opponent who observes that it will fall short of his target. Such failure to react sets the stage for a false lunge which is immediately followed by a straight lunge. This attack often succeeds because the defender has momentarily relaxed and believes the lunge is not a threat when in fact the real lunge can now be executed from a fairly close distance. The proper tempo should be a rather slow, nonthreatening false lunge followed without pause by a fast full lunge.

During any false actions, the attacker is vulnerable to some form of counterattack. Therefore, it is important that the sword arm never be "locked" so that a parry can be made quickly.

Finally, if you realize that your opponent is probing your defense with some false lunges, you can feed him some false responses. For example, if he makes a simple straight feinting action, you can react with a deliberately wide parry four. This will encourage the attacker to attempt a disengagement attack to your outside line, an attack for which you are ready. All this assumes that you are capable of differentiating between the opponent's false and real movements.

26. Advance Lunge

This is a lunge which immediately follows an advance.

Use

Many fencers take a step backward whenever they are attacked causing the attacker's lunge to fall short of the target. Against such an opponent, the attacker should make up the distance by taking a step forward just before lunging. The advance lunge should also be used against opponents who maintain a distance that is longer than the attacker can cover with a lunge.

Execution

Combine the advance and the lunge into a continuous forward movement. While the advance is being made, extend the sword arm so that the lunge can be made immediately. There should be no pause between the advance and the lunge once the combined movement has been learned. Any type of blade action can be used in conjunction with the advance lunge. If a compound attack such as a one-two is being made, the feint should be made during the advance.

Common Faults

Failing to extend the sword arm during the advance. Pausing between the advance and the lunge. Taking too long a step during the advance and not having room to make a full lunge.

Drills

1. Take one step back from your normal lunging distance. Practice the straight advance lunge with the partner offering no opposition. Later, practice the advance lunge while executing either a disengagement or a one-two. This requires close cooperation between partners.

2. From normal lunging distance, the defender takes a step to the rear while the attacker makes a simple advance lunge in anticipa-

tion of a retreat by his partner. If a disengagement is to be added, the attacker makes a straight thrust during the advance and disengages as the lunge begins. Meanwhile, the defending partner will parry the feint *after* having made his retreat.

Note

A variation of the advance lunge is the *ballestra* in which the fencer does a low forward jump with both feet and then lunges. The ballestra is too difficult for beginners and many experienced fencers never use it because they prefer the control afforded by the advance lunge.

27. Counterparry

This is a circular movement of the blade which is used to parry direct or disengagement attacks.

Use

If a defender were always to use only the simple parries four and six, the attacker would soon learn to expect and deceive these parries. A counterparry adds variety to the defense and makes it more difficult for an attacker to predict the type of parry that will be used against him.

Execution

The counterparry number six is probably the most useful for beginners and will be described here. The counterparry four can be learned by reversing instructions given here for the countersix. After engaging in fourth position, the defender will open his line by moving his blade a few inches to the right. As the attacker makes a straight lunge, the defender makes a clockwise circle with his foil thereby passing under the attacking blade and carrying it to a parry six position.

Against disengagements, start with a closed sixth line, and when the attacker attempts to disengage his blade into your open fourth line, make a clockwise circle with your foil, pass underneath the opponent's blade, and return his blade to the original sixth line of engagement. The sword hand should not move very much during this parry, since it is already in the sixth position.

The counterparry takes longer to execute than does a simple parry and it may be necessary to take a short retreat to gain time while parrying.

Common Faults

Executing the parry by rotating the forearm instead of only the foil. Waiting too long to initiate the parry and thereby being touched. Pulling the arm back to gain time while making the parry instead of taking a step back.

Note

The riposte following a counterparry is the same as that made following a simple parry. However, some fencers make the counterparry six and the riposte in a single action when they feel certain they can predict the attack that will be used. This is often a successful defense, but the beginner must concentrate on first completing his parry before making a riposte.

The discussion of Skill 25 also applies here. If the attacker can be led to believe that your next defense will be a simple parry, he can be surprised by your use of a counterparry. The essence of an effective defensive game is *unpredictability*. While simple parries are reflexive, counterparries are premeditated and used for specific tactical purposes.

28. Double

This is a compound attack used to avoid a counterparry.

Use

If the attacker has reason to believe that his opponent is going to use a counterparry, he must prepare to use a double if he hopes to penetrate to the target.

Execution

With both partners in sixth position, the first movement of the double is exactly the same as the first movement of the one-two. The defender has a line open into which the attacker makes a feint of a straight thrust. This causes the defender to use his counterparry, and as he does so, the attacker moves his foil point in a small counterclockwise circle around the parrying blade and lunges. Both blades should travel in the same direction and the speed of the defender's counterparry will determine the speed with which the double can be made. It is the attacker's responsibility to avoid any contact of blades.

Ideally, the defender's counterparry should be anticipated so that the double can be made with the lunge. However, the beginner should feint while remaining in the on-guard position and should lunge with the execution of the double.

Common Faults

Failing to extend the sword arm fully during the feint and thus failing to convince the opponent that there is a threat. Holding the feint so long that the defender succeeds in parrying the feint. Using the entire arm to move the foil point thus making an unnecessarily large circle. Making the double at a speed slower or faster than the speed of the defender's parry and thereby colliding with his blade instead of avoiding it.

Drill

As in the drill for the one-two, it is best to learn to do the double in a controlled drill. Begin with the defender in sixth position.

	Attacker	*Defender*
Step 1.	Feint into fourth line; no lunge.	No reaction; stay in sixth.
Step 2.	Execute double; lunge.	Counterparry six; allow self to be touched.
Step 3.	Return to on-guard position.	Return to on-guard position.

As the partners learn to work together, the double can be practiced without pause and at bout speed. There should be no contact of blades once the attack begins. When some proficiency is achieved, try the double with an advance lunge. The defending partner cooperates by first stepping back and then counterparrying. The attacker steps forward while extending his arm to feint and then doubles as he lunges.

29. Beat Attack

This is a sharp striking of the opponent's blade with the intention of deflecting it.

Use

When a defender has his sword arm extended so that his point is threatening, the attacker may use a beat to momentarily knock the blade aside so that he can obtain right of way to attack.

Execution

To make a beat in fourth, start in sixth position and relax the last three fingers of the sword hand so that a gap appears between the handle and the palm of the hand. Quickly contract the fingers in such a way as to bring your blade horizontally to the left into a forceful contact with the defender's blade. For the beat to be effective, the blades should meet at about their midpoints. Follow the beat with an extension of the sword arm and a lunge. The beat gives right of way only if the lunge is made immediately afterward. If the lunge is delayed, the defender may bring his point back into a threatening position and regain right of way.

Common Faults

Failing to use the middle of the blade to make the beat and thus making a weak beat. Drawing the blade back to get additional power for the beat, thereby telegraphing your intention.

Drills

As an exercise, partners engage in fourth position and alternately beat one another's blades. As your partner strikes your blade, relax the grip of your last three fingers and allow your handle to pivot between your thumb and forefinger. To make your own beat, smartly close the last three fingers, and return your blade into contact with that of your opponent. Do not allow the relaxing fingers to lose contact with the handle at any time.

The beats can be varied in speed, in strength, and in rhythm. This exercise is also excellent for helping to develop finger play so necessary to the French style of fencing.

Combine the beat drill with advances and retreats to develop coordination between the hand and the feet. The beat in sixth can also be practiced; but since finger play is not used for this beat, it is not valuable as a drill. The sixth beat is simply a backhand slap using the hand rather than the fingers to move the blade.

Try the beat attack against a partner who grips his foil tightly and has his arm extended. Your attack should be a continous sequence of beat, extend, and lunge. It is likely that as you land your touch your partner's blade will rebound into line and you will also be touched. However, the right of way is yours since you removed his threatening point momentarily and lunged without hesitation.

Discussion

One problem with teaching the beat to beginners is that they tend to overuse it. A beat used in combination with a false lunge is a good way to feel out a new opponent, and you may thus learn a great deal about his skill, strength, speed, and reflexes.

Finally, a defensive beat in fourth can be an effective form of parry. The parries learned in Skills 18 and 19 are called "opposition" parries in which the hand and foil move laterally to meet and block an attack. If a fencer is in sixth position and is attacked with a direct lunge, he can make a beat parry four while keeping his hand in sixth position.

The advantage of the beat parry is that it is quite fast because of the high velocity achieved by the end of the blade. This speed results in a sharp blow to the attacking blade and can deflect it farther than can an opposition parry. Also, since the sword hand does not move much, it does not uncover a line into which a disengagement can be easily made. To succeed with this parry, the fencer must be able to maintain good distance, otherwise his parry will be late and will meet the defender's blade high up on the forte or strong part where it cannot easily deflect the attack. Opposition parries are to be preferred when distance cannot be maintained or when the opponent has a very strong attack.

30. Beat and Disengagement

Use

When it is found that the opponent parries reflexively to a beat on his blade, you may use the beat as a feint and follow it with a disengagement under the opponent's parry effort.

Execution

Beat from the on-guard position and disengage into the line that is being opened when your partner responds to your beat with his parry.

Common Faults

Extending the sword arm during the beat. Pausing between the beat and disengagement thus giving the opponent time to parry the attack.

Note

The beat could also be followed by a one-two attack or by a double. The choice would depend on the expected reaction of the opponent.

31. Attacks to the Low Line

These are any attacks which terminate on the part of the target that is below the normal hand level of the opponent.

Use

Since the full foil target is vulnerable, the attacker should seek any target open to him. Low line attacks may be direct or may follow one or more feints to other lines.

Execution

A straight lunge to the low line is made pretty much in the same manner as any other straight lunge. Some fencers prefer to pronate the hand (turn the knuckles up) for low attacks to get better fixation on the target and to avoid the opponent's arm.

Many variations are possible. If the opponent has a good low line defense, it will be necessary to use feints. A feint may be made into the high line and followed with a lunge to the low area. A feint may be first made into the low line and followed with a high-line attack. A double being made against a countersix parry can be terminated in the low line simply by not quite completing the double which ordinarily would be completed in the high line.

Common Faults

Pronating the hand may cause the fencer to lose accuracy with his point. In disengaging from a high to a low line or vice versa, a fencer may use too much arm movement instead of guiding his blade with his fingers and hand.

Discussion

Although the high target area is the largest and the most frequently attacked, it is also the area that most fencers learn to defend best. Attacks to the low lines can be successful even against experienced fencers. Simply threatening to attack his low line can cause problems for an opponent.

All students should wear trousers when practicing low line attacks, and male competitive fencers wear cup supporters in addition for greater safety.

32. Parry Number Seven

This is a defensive action which deflects an attack made into the inside (left) low line.

Use

Since the full foil target is vulnerable, the defender must be able to parry attacks to his low target area.

Execution

Lower your point to a level a few inches below the hand and move the hand and foil to the left just far enough to deflect the attacking blade away from the target. The hand position is essentially the same as that for the parry four.

When the defender's sword hand is already in the fourth position at the beginning of the attack, his blade will have to follow an inward semicircular path to the parry seven position. This half-circle will be more likely to pick up the attacking blade than will a simple lowering of the point (Fig. 16).

Common Faults

Lowering the hand in making the parry. Extending the arm or drawing it back in making the parry. Turning the knuckles up.

33. Parry Number Eight

This is a defensive action which deflects an attack made into the outside (right) low line.

Use

Since the full foil target is vulnerable, the defender must be able to parry attacks to his low target area.

Execution

Lower the point to a level a few inches below the hand and move the hand and foil to the right just far enough to deflect the attacking blade away from the target. The hand position is essentially the same as that described for the parry six.

When the defender's sword hand is already in the sixth position at the beginning of the attack, his blade will have to follow an inward semicircular path to the parry eight position. This half-circle will be more likely to pick up the attacking blade than will a simple lowering of the point.

Common Faults

Lowering the hand, extending the arm, or drawing back the hand in making the parry.

Note

The riposte from a low-line parry is often made to the opponent's low line, but it can be made into the high line.

The low line parries may be used with surprising effect against anticipated disengagement and one-two attacks. Since the attacking blade must pass under yours, by lowering your point and making the appropriate parry seven or eight you will block the attacker's disengagement effort. The riposte would then follow your meeting of the opponent's blade.

Parry Seven   *Parry Eight*

Figure 16.

34. Other Parries

This book has discussed the simple parries four, six, seven, and eight and the counterparries six and four. When combined with retreats, these parries are more than sufficient for effective defense.

There are four other parries that have occasional value to the advanced fencer. Parry one defends the entire inside line. The palm

Hicol

Low

out side

inside

0 sixte

3 Tierce

2 seconde

8 octave

1

4 quarte

1 Prime Hicol

7 septime

5 quinte Low

n side

faces the opponent and its main drawback is that the sword hand is awkwardly placed for the riposte. Parry two defends the outside low line, as does the parry eight, and can be a very strong and effective parry if the blade is not swung too far. Parry three performs the same function as the parry six in defending the high outside target. The riposte is more difficult than from the sixth parry, but it allows for some maneuverability at close quarters. The parry five resembles a parry four made with the hand low, and it defends the inside low target.

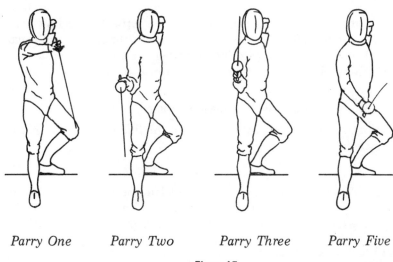

Parry One   Parry Two   Parry Three   Parry Five

Figure 17.

35. Redoublement

A redoublement is a second attempt to hit an opponent when the first attack has missed or was parried and no counterattack has been begun by the opponent.

Use

Often when an attack misses or is parried, the opponent hesitates or neglects to riposte. During such a lapse by the defender, the attacker may remain in the lunge and make a quick, short thrust.

Execution

There is no particular method for making a redoublement because it is not so much a specific action as it is a description of an act. Usually a redoublement is done by slightly withdrawing the foil and immediately thrusting a second time into the original or any other line.

Common Faults

Trying to do a redoublement during the normal sequence of fencing instead of in the absence of action by the opponent. For example, if the redoublement is attempted while the opponent is making an immediate riposte, the riposte has the right of way.

Note

This movement is sometimes called a *remise* but technically a remise is a replacement of the point, usually after it is initially parried, in the same line and with no additional arm or blade actions. A redoublement may involve a scoring attempt into any line.

36. Disengage Riposte

This is an indirect riposte made into the line opposite to that of the parry.

Use

Very often a direct riposte does not land because the opponent is quick in covering his line after his attack has been parried. An indirect riposte may be used to score in such a case.

Execution

After completing the parry, disengage your blade into the opposite line and then extend to score your touch. If the opponent remains in his lunge, it is important to move only your blade and not your arm during the disengagement. Then extend after clearing the defender's arm. If the opponent recovers and parries, your riposte is made in the same manner as a disengage lunge (Skill 23).

Common Faults

Extending while disengaging. Making the disengagement wide or slowly thereby giving the attacker an opportunity to recover or to resume his attack.

Drills

The attacking partner lunges and is parried. He remains in his lunge and closes his line in anticipation of a direct riposte. The defender follows his parry with a disengage riposte but does not lunge.

37. Point in Line

This is simply an on-guard stance with the arm fully extended and the point threatening the opponent. It takes advantage of one of the rules of Right of Way which states that if a fencer has a threatening point in line the opponent must first remove the point to gain the right to attack.

Use

By taking this position, you put the burden of removing your threat upon your opponent. This is a tactical decision on your part, and you must have some plan in mind to deal with the probable attack on your blade. It is unlikely that your adversary will ignore your blade threatening and make a direct lunge onto your point.

Execution

Before your opponent begins an attack, extend your sword arm and direct your tip at some part of his valid target, either high or low. You need not remain stationary and may advance, retreat, or even lunge without losing your right of way. You may not flex your arm or move your point away from threatening the target.

The point can be placed in line against an opponent who begins an attack ahead of you but does so in a manner which does not give him right of way. For instance, he may have his arm bent, or he may make very wide blade movements that do not present a threat to your target. This skill should not be confused with the *stop hit* which is a form of counterattack that must actually hit before the final phase of the attack begins. The stop hit is an active stroke by the defender whereas the point in line is a passive act.

Common Faults

Flexing the sword arm while being attacked. Extending the arm after the attack has been initiated against you. Aiming your blade away from valid target while being attacked.

Note

Knowing full well that your opponent will be attempting a beat attack against your extended blade, you can frustrate him by keeping your distance by retreating whenever he appears ready to attack. If he telegraphs his beats, you can try to avoid his beat by disengaging your blade without bending your arm and thus retain right of way. Of course, you can always parry his beat attack if necessary.

Tactically, you might choose this position because your normal defense has not worked and you need some time to think. Putting your point in line may momentarily present a problem for your opponent, and you may see a noticeable change in his game as he ponders his next move. This is often an ideal time to launch your own attack as he may be unprepared to defend.

When you are fencing someone who has a point in line, there are several things to consider. If you are leading the bout, there is no need to attack, and your opponent cannot remain passive very long if he expects to win. You may try a beat false lunge to observe his reactions. If you suspect that he plans to disengage against your beat, then deliberately telegraph a wide beat and, when he makes his disengagement, beat a second time and lunge.

38. Cutover (Coupé)

This simple attack is a disengagement in which the blade goes over rather than under the defender's blade.

Use

While the cutover serves the same purpose as the disengagement, the timing involved is different enough to enable it to penetrate some styles of defense.

Execution

Raise your point just high enough to clear the opponent's point, extend into the opposite line, and lunge. The point is raised through a combination of wrist movement and slight bending of the elbow.

Common Faults

Drawing the sword arm back more than is necessary. Raising the hand to assist in making the cutover. Delaying the action at the peak of the cutover instead of bringing the point into line immediately.

Note

The cutover can be combined with other movements. For example a cutover can be followed by a disengagement under, or two successive cutovers can be used instead of a one-two attack.

The cutover (coupé) is often effective when done with an advance lunge. If this attack is used excessively, the defender may anticipate it and score with a stop hit while the attacker's blade is being raised to cut over.

39. Invitation

This is any position taken by a fencer which exposes his target deliberately and tempts the opponent to try to hit it.

Use

An occasional opponent may be reluctant to attack you either because he is fearful of your defensive ability or because he himself is strong defensively and is awaiting your attack. Such an opponent may be made to attack by offering him an opportunity that is too good to ignore.

Execution

A common invitation is to assume the eighth position thus leaving the high line open. Another type of invitation is that of closing the distance while exposing some target. The invitation can be so obvious as to actually be a dare, or it can be subtle enough that the opponent is unaware that you are deliberately opening your target.

Common Faults

Making the invitation so wide that you cannot parry the attack you have drawn. Responding predictably from any given invitation position. Getting too close while inviting.

Note

The success of the invitation is determined not only by whether it draws an attack, but also by whether the defender is capable of parrying the attack. It is important, therefore, to take into account the opponent's speed and length of lunge. From the eighth position, an attack into your high line can be deflected with either a parry four or a parry six.

Basically, any fencer on-guard is always open somewhere as only one line can be closed at a time. Such openings are invitations only when they are deliberate. The defender hopes that his opponent will "take the bait" and attack a specific target area even though other areas are also open at that moment. Of course, there is no point in giving an invitation if you have no trap in mind.

The best invitations are those given rather suddenly in the hopes that the opponent will react by reflex rather than by reason.

Another category of invitation involves some form of obvious blade action or a pattern of actions. You might, for instance, set up a rhythmic sequence of slow wide beats. If your opponent decides to deceive one of these beats with a disengage lunge, you are prepared to parry and riposte.

Often you can create the illusion of a wide-open target when in fact you are no more vulnerable than if you were in a normal on-guard stance. In the eighth position, your high line appears to be quite open, but you can make a very fast semicircular beat parry of either four or six without even moving your hand. Here again, if you can get your opponent into a frame of mind set upon solving the problem of your invitation, you may find him ripe for an attack of your own.

Against a fencer who uses invitations, the false lunge is your best tactic. It often "springs the trap" and forces the defender back into a conventional stance. As you gain experience, it is often possible to second guess the opponent's plans and do a feint disengage against his parry.

40. Varieties of Defense

Use

Knowledge of four simple parries and two counterparries does not insure a sound defense. If the fencer makes his parries in any predictable pattern, the attacker can anticipate the parries and successfully deceive them.

Execution

The basic approach must be one of unpredictability of the defense. Parries must be mixed as much as possible and retreats employed defensively so that the opponent will not know whether the defender will parry, which parry he will use, or if he will retreat.

Against a straight lunge, it is possible to step back, to counterparry, or to simple parry.

Against a disengage lunge from a closed sixth line into your open fourth, it is possible to parry four, to counterparry six, or to parry eight. If the parry eight is used, the defender would be *breaking the line* or would, in other words, be using a low line parry against a high line attack.

Against a one-two attack made from closed six to four and back to six, it is possible to counterparry six, to parry four and six, to parry eight against the feint, to parry seven against the second disengage, or to parry four and counter four.

Note

It may be seen that there is more than one parry that may be used against any given attack. It is not necessary to use each and every possible parry, but it is important to present a problem to the opponent who is trying to analyze your defense.

41. Flèche

This is a quick attack in which the rear leg moves ahead of the front leg. It is the French word for arrow.

Use

When the distance kept by an opponent is such that it is difficult to reach him with a lunge, the flèche may be effectively employed. It is more commonly used by sabremen than by foilsmen because the normal distance between sabre fencers is greater than that kept in foil.

Execution

As the arm is extended, the weight is shifted forward onto the right leg. When the body has leaned forward to the point that balance is being lost, the right leg drives the fencer forward and the fencer moves into a near dive towards the opponent. The left leg crosses in front of the right leg to prevent the fencer from falling, and this is followed by a short run as a result of the momentum gathered. The entire movement must be made explosively but smoothly. It might be compared with a sprinter starting a one hundred yard dash.

Any of the attacks may be performed during the flèche. It is also possible to flèche with the riposte. There are a variety of movements which can be made just prior to making the flèche. For example, a flèche can be preceded by a false lunge, by an advance, or even by a retreat.

Common Faults

Accelerating rather than starting at full speed. Standing up from the on-guard position and running rather than leaning extremely far forward just before running. Flèching from too great a distance or against an opponent who is already retreating. Flèching from a distance close enough to warrant using the more controllable lunge. Telegraphing by crouching or leaning just before the flèche.

Note

The flèche is potentially dangerous when used by an untrained fencer. One hazard is that the flèche could result in violent collisions—often two beginners will flèche simultaneously and run into one another with great force. There is also the danger that a beginner will hold his weapon very firmly and the force of the flèche might cause the blade to snap. Every fencer who uses the flèche should be trained to relax his grip as he makes his touch. Generally, the flèche should not be taught to beginners.

Figure 18. Flèche.

42. Other Attacks on the Blade

Aside from the beat, there are a number of actions that can be taken against an opposing blade the most common of which are the bind, glide, and pressure.

Use

Actions on the blade may be necessitated by a threatening point in line or by a concern for the opponent's remise.

Execution

Pressure: Engage your opponent's blade in fourth, and by using your fingers and wrist press hard enough to momentarily expel his blade and give you the right to lunge. The effect is the same as that caused by a beat, but the pressure requires virtually no hand movement and is therefore less apt to be telegraphed. As with the beat, the fingers have a relaxed grip on the handle, and their forceful flexion will bring the handle into the palm causing the blade to press the opponent's blade. Since a pressure usually brings a blade response, a pressure and disengagement is an effective attack.

Bind: This must be done against extended arms only. Place your blade in fourth engagement but with your forte against the forward third (foible) of your opponent's blade. Immediately lower your point to the side opposite that of your engagement, and move your hand to the right while extending your arm and lunging. The effect of this sequence of actions is to control and deflect the opposing blade while scoring a touch yourself. Your blade must be in constant contact with your opponent's weapon. Your hand remains high, but your touch should land on the lower target. The bind may also follow a parry four, especially if the attacker is strong and tries to replace his point with some opposition.

Glide: When faced with a point in line, you may make what amounts to a disengagement and lunge with strong opposition. Begin by moving your point beneath the opponent's extended blade. Then lift your hand and weapon up and to the right while also lunging. If done correctly, you will score very high on the chest and deflect the opposing blade off of your own target. As with the bind, try to get forte against foible so as to have the advantage in leverage.

Discussion

Blade attacks other than the beat are difficult for beginners and are not an essential part of any course. The chance to score is not worth the risks of mistiming, failing to control the opposing blade, and being resisted.

Against an opponent who likes to attack the blade, take an invitation position in eighth so that he cannot take action on it. Or keep your blade in motion so that the opponent cannot contact it. If a bind is being made, you may resist. If a glide is being made, lift your hand high and the attack will go over your shoulder.

STUDY QUESTIONS FOR CHAPTER 3

1. What advantage is there to closing a line?
2. In what situation is a double used?
3. Fencer A lunges and B parries successfully. The riposte by B hits off-target. A then continues with a remise that touches B on the chest. What will be the director's decision?

4. In the one-two attack, what is the function of the first dis-engagement?

5. Why is a direct riposte to the chest difficult following a parry six?

6. Give two situations in which an advance lunge might have to be used?

7. Which target area is protected by each of the simple parries that were discussed?

8. When making a counterparry four, in which direction does the blade rotate?

9. How is a closing of a line different from a parry?

10. Is timing or execution more important in the stop hit? Why?

11. When would a disengage riposte be more appropriate than a direct riposte?

12. Describe the valid targets for all three weapons.

chapter 4
Elementary Bouts

After having been restricted to drills since the first class period, the student will naturally be anxious to fence and try out his skills. For many students, the transition from cooperative exercises to combat is not easy. Feeling awkward and unsure of what to do and being pressured by an opponent who is trying his best to beat him, the beginner may regress to some primitive actions. Therefore, these early bouts should be short and alternated with review drills. There should be no emphasis on winning, but, rather, the student should consider his bouts as a sort of laboratory exercise in which he has some opportunity to experiment and learn.

It is actually more difficult for a beginner to fence another beginner than it is to fence someone slightly more advanced who is trained to respond "correctly." The wide and wild actions of a novice opponent present a real problem to which the best answer is patience. With experience, you will learn to deal with difficult styles.

To help yourself and your opponent in practice bouts, there should be a short pause after each touch is scored. The fencer who was hit should acknowledge the touch and perhaps point to the spot where the touch landed. Touches made off the target should likewise be acknowledged even though no points or penalties are involved. If both fencers were hit during a single flurry of action (called a phrase), they should attempt to determine who had the right of way.

You may find it more comfortable at first to fence a few bouts in which there is a designated attacker and defender. In every respect, these would be normal bouts except that only one partner is permitted to take offensive actions while the other may score only on ripostes.

Tactics

When first facing a new opponent, there should be a short feeling-out period. Keep your distance and make occasional false lunges to probe your opponent's reactions. Do not make the common error of attacking without having some notion of what to expect in the way of a defense.

Other things being equal, the attacking fencer has the best chance of winning. Offensive skills are easier to learn than defensive skills, and the new fencer must attack at every opportunity. The attack need not be complex, and, in fact, most novices ordinarily make compound actions that are not suitable to the situation.

If some basic concepts had to be set down, they would include:

1. Make the simplest attack that has a chance to succeed. If it fails, then try the next more complex action as, for example, when a simple lunge is parried you would try a single disengagement on the next attack.

2. Whatever attack you make should conform to the expected defense; have a reason for what you do.

3. Even when you make the appropriate choice of attack, it must be made to blend with the opponent's movement speed. You seldom can act independently; the defense dictates what the offense must do.

4. Rely more on retreats than on parries. The parries will then have some surprise effect, and you will be parrying because you are ready to rather than because you must. The retreat should be your immediate response to any unusual offensive moves against you. In other words, when in doubt, get out.

5. Successful parries do not score points for you. You must riposte. Even if your riposte doesn't hit, the fact that you do riposte will prevent your opponent from making remises and redoublements.

6. Unless you are prepared to attack or defend, keep a distance greater than your opponent's lunge range. Once you are within lunge range, there is no need to advance further, but you must decide instantly whether to attack or step back out of distance.

7. Selecting the correct time to begin your attack is as important as the choice of attack. Whenever possible, begin your attack just as your opponent moves toward you with his sword arm still bent. Your chances of reaching are very good because an opponent moving forward has to stop and reverse direction in order to retreat. For the same reason, it is unwise to attack a fencer who is retreating or in good position to retreat. Be patient and select the best moment to attack.

Remember that fencing is combat and that your objective is simply to hit your opponent and not be hit yourself. What makes fencing fun and a challenge is that each opponent is different. Each will vary in skill, height, speed, aggressiveness, coordination, experience, intelligence, and strength. For that reason, you must be prepared to fence each new opponent a bit differently. You may have to modify skills you have learned to cope with a difficult style; you may have to even invent a movement to solve a particular problem. Beginners often have trouble when fencing a left-handed opponent, and the solution is to practice frequently with left-handers.

You will expend a lot of energy needlessly at first, but with practice you will be more relaxed and your movements will have more purpose. It might be said that your fencing will go through three stages of development: first you will learn to control your body and legs; then you will learn to use your blade offensively and defensively; finally, after the first two stages have become more or less automatic, your brain will be free to concentrate on your opponent and to devise ways and means of defeating him. The fun really begins when you reach the third stage of learning.

For the More Advanced Student

If you are to continue developing as a fencer, you will need a combination of regular instruction and a good deal of bout experience. Join a club if possible, and enter local competitions when your coach feels that you are ready.

Once you have achieved the usual blade skills, you need time for your tactical sense to develop. Don't hesitate to try out your own ideas, and be prepared to make mistakes and lose touches. How fast you develop depends on how effectively you study, how often you practice, and the quality of your practice partners.

To supplement your instruction, read the rules book and a variety of fencing books. Observe good fencers at every opportunity, and note their tactics and movements.

Because this is a beginning text, the full range of tactics available to an advanced fencer will not be discussed. However, some basic considerations are appropriate to list.

1. If your tactics have been working and you are winning the bout, do not change. Suppose that a disengage lunge has worked twice already. It is certainly a good gamble to try it again soon in that bout. If you have been scoring with ripostes, then you should continue to allow your opponent to do the attacking for the remainder of the bout.

2.   On the other hand, if you are losing the bout, you must change your tactics. Perhaps you have been too defensive, then take the offense. If you cannot attack because your opponent is more aggressive than you are, perhaps you can assume a different guard stance such as a point in line or an invitation position.

3.   Try to manipulate your opponent; get him to play your game. Keep him off balance with false lunges, and give him a variety of problems to solve.

4.   Use the whole fencing strip. Give ground when necessary but regain it at every opportunity. Try not to get backed to the end of the strip where you will be forced to change your game plan.

5.   Learn to analyze every action in a bout, the unsuccessful as well as the successful. The director's description of the phrase may provide some important information.

6.   Listen carefully to the director's analysis. If he seems to favor one movement over another, adjust your own game accordingly. As in all sports, there is a range of officiating quality, and it does no good to complain. A smart athlete adjusts so as to get the favorable decisions.

7.   Keep a distance to suit your game. Against some opponents, a rapid closing of distance will force an error. At other times, if you stay at long range you might frustrate your opponent into making an advancing attack which you may find easier to parry. Simply maintaining a "correct" distance at all times is not in itself enough. The tactical use of both open and covert changes of distance should be practiced.

8.   Think about what you will do when you find yourself in a bout with only twenty seconds left to fence. The three score situations are that you are leading, trailing, or tied. Naturally, if you are leading you hope to run out the clock and will therefore give ground to use up time. If you are behind, you can expect your opponent to stall and you have no choice but to attack without much preparation. Several attacks can be made in the space of twenty seconds. With the score tied, the pressure is not so great to act but you are fencing for one touch and it is helpful if you have been doing a running diagnosis through the bout. Ask yourself how you scored the previous touches and also how your opponent scored his, because he may well try again what worked earlier and you had best be prepared.

9.   Go to each practice with something specific you wish to improve. After the day's practice, you should be able to cite what you learned and how you have improved. In the same way, every bout you fence in practice is an opportunity to learn.

There is an old saying that fencing is a conversation with blades. Each time that you make some action, you are in a real sense talking to your opponent. Just as very young children chatter a great deal, so do novice fencers make many meaningless, random "statements" with the blade. As language develops with age, so does the fencer's ability to debate with his foil. The comments that he makes now have more impact on the opponent. The feint instead of being a mere blur to the eye now seems to say "Here I come, parry me or else."

Just as you don't enjoy the company of a bore, you will dislike a lengthy bout with a dull, unimaginative opponent. But cross blades with someone who varies his game, lays traps, and senses your every move, then you'll have found real dialogue and your whole being will be stimulated by the fight.

Etiquette

Before putting on your mask, salute your opponent and when he has returned the salute you may then put on your mask. During a practice bout, each fencer is obligated to call touches against himself but never against his opponent.

In competitive bouts, the officials will determine right of way and the contestants may not try to influence the decisions with any comments or gestures. However, you may politely inquire about a particular interpretation of a phrase and you are always permitted to protest an erroneous application of rules. A display of temper upon losing a bout is considered to be bad manners but it is also non-productive and a reflection upon your coach.

At the conclusion of any bout, the universal practice is to shake hands with the ungloved hand after removal of the mask. By custom, spectators refrain from booing or cheering during the fencing. The director has to be able to hear the electric apparatus buzzer and certain signals from the scorekeeper, and if the crowd noise interferes, the director has the power to request silence.

STUDY QUESTIONS FOR CHAPTER 4

1. What are two things that a beginner might do incorrectly in making the feint part of the one-two?
2. What is a phrase?
3. In what ways can a false attack be helpful to the beginner?
4. What is the best time to attack an opponent?

5. Why do you think a left-hander presents a problem?
6. With which hand does a right-handed fencer shake hands at the end of a bout?

chapter 5
Rules and Officiating

Valid Target Area

In foil fencing, the torso is the valid target. In front, the target extends from the top of the collar down to the creases formed between the thigh and the lower abdomen. In back, the target extends from the top of the collar down to a line connecting the tops of the hip bones. The electric foil vest is cut to exactly cover the torso.

Figure 19. Valid foil target area (unshaded).

Fencing Boundaries

Competitive bouts are fought on strips measuring about six feet by forty-six feet and contestants must remain within those limits. The strip is usually several feet longer than the end boundaries to allow room for a fencer to retreat out of bounds without danger of tripping over the edge of the strip. For some meets it may be acceptable to use masking tape to mark out the boundaries directly on the gymnasium floor, but in competitions with electric weapons, grounded copper mesh strips are used whenever possible.

During a foil bout, when a fencer is retreating and his rear foot reaches the warning line, the bout is halted by the director and the fencer is informed that he is under warning. When the bout resumes, should the fencer then continue retreating and cross the rear boundary with both feet, a touch is awarded against him. The warning is removed by the scoring of a touch by either fencer or by the regaining of ground up to the center line.

Whenever a fencer leaves a side boundary with both feet, he is replaced one meter back of the point from which he left the mat. Anytime one foot leaves the side of the strip, the bout is halted and the fencers replaced on the strip with no penalty.

A fencer who steps off the side of the strip with both feet may not score a touch against his opponent, but he can be scored upon by an immediate riposte.

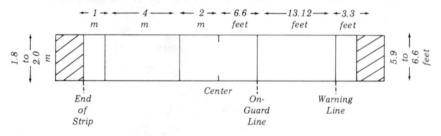

Figure 20. Foil strip measurements. Metric units (meters) are given on the left, English units (feet) on the right.

Scoring

A valid touch is one in which the tip arrives on the target in a forward movement and momentarily fixes. The pressure needed to depress the push-button tip of an electric foil is 500 grams, and an equivalent force would be expected in nonelectric foil. Any contact by the side of the blade would not register on the electric apparatus, and of course a judge in nonelectric foil would ignore such a flat hit just as he would a complete miss.

When a touch is made on invalid target area such as the arm or mask, the bout is stopped, the fencers are placed on-guard, and the bout is resumed. There are no penalties for off-target touches, but no other touches made in the same phrase are considered.

Touches awarded by the bout director are scored *against* the fencer who was hit. Thus, at any time during a bout, the fencer with the lowest score is leading. To win the bout, a fencer must score five points against his opponent. The final score can be anything from 5-0 to 5-4.

Time Limits

The time limits vary with the type of meet. Intercollegiate meets use a four minute time limit whereas a bout for five touches in a U.S.F.A. competition can last six minutes. In either case, a warning is given by the timekeeper when there is one minute remaining to fence. The clock starts running with the director's command to fence and stops with each command to halt.

If time elapses before five touches have been scored against one fencer, the bout is won by whomever is leading. Enough points are then added to the score of the loser to bring it up to five and a like number of points is added to the winner's score. Thus, if time expires with the score standing at 3-1, the final score will be recorded as 5-3. Should the score be tied when the time ran out, the score is raised to 4-4 and the fencers play for one decisive touch.

Official's Duties

Director: This is the head official in total charge of the bout. When the fencers have saluted and are prepared to fence, his first commands are "Ready? Fence." As the fencers move up and down the strip, the director also moves so as to maintain a position from which he can observe both fencers and all four judges or, in electric foil, the scoring box. If the scoring apparatus registers a touch or if any judges raise their hands, he calls "Halt" to stop the action.

He then reconstructs the phrase just completed, announces which fencer had right of way, and polls the judges to establish the materiality of a touch, i.e., whether a touch was observed. In the electric foil, the apparatus determines the materiality and the director decides the validity, that is, which fencer is to be awarded the point. The determination of right of way is the most important duty of the director. In nonelectric foil or in sabre, he also participates in the judgement of materiality.

Judge: In nonelectric foil, there are four judges, two on either side of the director. The two judges to the director's right are watching for touches made on the fencer to the director's left and vice versa. The main task of the judge is to raise a hand upon seeing a touch that lands *anywhere*, and, when polled by the director, the judge must be able to cast a vote as to what he thought happened in that phrase. If several exchanges took place in one phrase, the judge should be able to state the outcome of each.

The judge should take a position to the side and rear of the fencer for whom he is judging, and he should move with the fencer so as to keep a uniform view of the target and also to stay out of the way of a wild parry which might cause him injury. A judge is bound to be impartial even when a teammate is fencing.

The full jury is made up of the four judges and the director. In electric foil, the electric apparatus replaces the four judges but not the director.

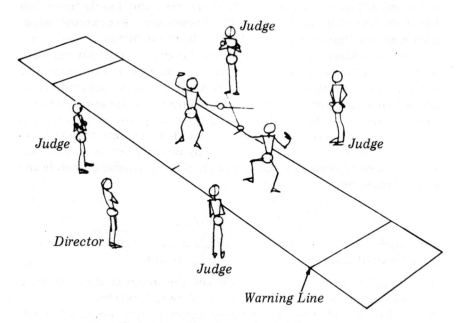

Figure 21. Positions of jury for nonelectric foil and for sabre.

Auxiliary Personnel

Scorekeeper: Each touch awarded is recorded in the proper place on the scoresheet and sometimes also on whatever visual scoreboard may be used for the spectators. Where no visual devices are available, the scorekeeper should call out the running score as he records each point. This will protect him in the event there is a mistake and it keeps everyone informed about the score. At the conclusion of the bout, the scorekeeper announces the final score, calls the names of the next two contestants, and announces the names of the on-deck fencers.

Timekeeper: The main duty of the timekeeper is to start the clock with the command "Fence" and stop the clock with the command "Halt." When one minute remains, the timekeeper holds up a hand to so inform the director who then warns the fencers. When time runs out, the timekeeper follows the agreed upon procedure, either calling out "Time," ringing a bell, blowing a whistle, or sounding a horn. This terminates the bout and no actions are considered following the timekeeper's signal. Most bouts end before time becomes a factor, but when they do not, the timekeeper's job becomes very important. Both timekeeper and scorekeeper sit at a table on the opposite side of the strip from the director.

Scoring Machine Operator: When the electric foil is being used, it is necessary for someone to operate the machine. His responsibility is to reset the machine after the director has had an opportunity to see which lights were on and to make a decision. He also resets the machine when the fencers are testing their weapons. When fencing is going on, the operator must keep his hands away from the machine.

While it is not to be desired, it may be necessary in some meets for one person to handle two jobs such as keep score and operate the scoring machine.

Method of Voting

Each member of the jury including the director has four possible types of votes regarding any touch attempt:

1. "Yes" is the vote if the judge saw the touch land on the valid target area with the foil tip having forward motion.
2. "No" is the vote if the judge believes that the touch either missed, hit flat, or was parried.
3. "Yes, but off target" is the vote if the judge saw the touch land on any but valid target area.
4. "Abstain" is the vote if the judge has no opinion about the action.

When a judge signals a touch by raising a hand, the director calls for a halt. After reconstructing the phrase for everyone's benefit, the director polls the judges. Beginning with the two judge's whose fencer had the initial right of way, the judges and director vote on the materiality of that specific action. If that action missed or was parried and the right of way passed to the other fencer, the director then votes with the other two judges regarding the return action. The director thus follows the action one step at a time until he determines which, if either, fencer is scored upon. It can be seen how important it is for the director to correctly visualize and remember each phrase.

If two fencers attack simultaneously, then neither has right of way, and if both landed touches, neither gets a touch. If an action had right of way but hit off target, all subsequent touches in that phrase are disregarded.

There will naturally be differences of opinion about the materiality of any given touch. The voting system gives each judge a vote worth one point and gives the director a vote worth one and a half points. Two judges in agreement can outvote a disagreeing director by a half-point margin. The director and one judge in agreement can outvote the remaining judge by a one and a half point margin. An abstention carries no point value in the judging and only the votes of the officials who have opinions will be tallied. If the vote results in a tie or no majority for one view, the decision is a "doubtful touch." Such a decision normally means nothing more is done and the fencers resume fencing. The table on page 73 summarizes most of the possible voting combinations and their outcomes.

Each time a touch is awarded, the fencers return to the on-guard lines before resuming. However, if the phrase analysis does not result in a touch award, the fencers remain where they were on the strip when the bout was halted.

In nonelectric foil, the contestants change sides when the leading fencer has scored three points. This change of sides equalizes any differences in lighting or judging quality. Incidentally, sabre fencing is judged in much the same manner as nonelectric foil, and sabre fencers also change sides at three touches.

Rules

Many of the rules of foil fencing have been discussed in various places through this text. Already explained were rules of right of way, time limits, strip boundaries, target areas, use of the unarmed hand, unnecessary roughness, and disarmings.

Voting Table for Touch Decisions in Non-electric Foil and Sabre

	Votes		Total		
Judge A (1 point)	Judge B (1 point)	Director (1½ points)	Ballot Points	Decision	Touch Awarded?
Yes	Yes	Yes	$3\frac{1}{2}$ - 0	Good touch	Yes
No	No	No	$3\frac{1}{2}$ - 0	No touch	No
Yes	No	No	$1 - 2\frac{1}{2}$	No touch	No
Yes	Yes	No	$2 - 1\frac{1}{2}$	Good touch	Yes
Yes	Abstain	No	$1 - 0 - 1\frac{1}{2}$	No touch	No
No	Abstain	Yes	$1 - 0 - 1\frac{1}{2}$	Good touch	Yes
Yes	No	Abstain	1 - 1 - 0	Doubtful touch	No
Off Target	Abstain	No	$1 - 0 - 1\frac{1}{2}$	No touch	No
Off Target	Yes	No	$1 - 1 - 1\frac{1}{2}$	Doubtful touch	No
Off Target	No	Abstain	1 - 1 - 0	Doubtful touch	No
Off Target	Off Target	Yes	$2 - 1\frac{1}{2}$	Off Target	No
Abstain	Abstain	Abstain	0 - 0 - 0	Doubtful touch	No
Yes	Abstain	Abstain	1 - 0 - 0	Good touch	Yes
Abstain	Abstain	No	$0 - 0 - 1\frac{1}{2}$	No touch	No

There are a number of rules specific to the electric foil with which we cannot be concerned here. There are also a number of rules which apply to both standard and electric foil, one of which pertains to infighting. When two fencers come into close quarters, they are allowed to continue fighting so long as they are able to freely use their foils and the director can follow the action. If the fencers reverse positions on the strip, the bout is halted and they are replaced in their original positions. Body contact (corps-à-corps) is not allowed and draws the director's warning. No right of way exists during infighting and the point goes to the first person to score.

Some excerpts from the 1982 U.S.F.A. Rules Book:

2. Observance of the phrase d'armes (fencing phrase)
233 (a) Every attack, that is, every initial offensive action, correctly executed, must be parried or completely avoided. . . .

To judge the correctness of an attack, the following points must be considered:
1. The simple attack, direct or indirect, . . . is correctly executed when the extending of the arm with the point threatening the valid surface precedes the beginning of the lunge or fleche.
2. The composite attack . . . is correctly executed when the arm extends in the presentation of the first feint, with the point threatening the valid surface, without withdrawal of the arm during the execution of the successive movements. . . .
To judge the priority (right-of-way) of an attack in the analysis of the phrase d'armes, the following points must be considered:
6. If the attack begins when the opponent is "in line", that is, with the arm extended and the point threatening the valid surface, the attacker must, as a preliminary, deflect the opposing weapon.
7. If, in searching for the opposing blade to deflect it, the attacker does not find the blade (derobement), the right-of-way passes to his opponent.

3. Judging
237 In applying these fundamental conventions of the foil, the Director must judge as follows:
Whenever, in a phrase d'armes, the fencers are both touched simultaneously, there has been either a simultaneous action or a double touch.
The former is the result of simultaneous conception and execution of the attack by both fencers; in this case, the touches given are annulled for both fencers, even if one of them has touched an invalid surface.
The double touch, on the contrary, is the result of a faulty action on the part of one of the fencers.
Consequently, if there is not a period of fencing time between the two touches:
1. The fencer attacked is alone counted as touched—
(a) if he makes a stop into a simple attack;
(b) if, instead of parrying, he attempts to avoid being touched, and fails;

(c) if, after a successful parry, he pauses for a moment—which gives his opponent the right to resume his attack (redoublement, remise, or reprise);

(d) if, on a composite attack, he makes a stop without having the advantage of a period of fencing time;

(e) if, being in line (arm extended and point threatening a valid surface), after a beat or a taking of the blade which deflects his weapon, he attacks or replaces his blade in line instead of parrying a direct thrust made by the attacker.

2. The attacker alone is counted as touched—

(a) if he starts his attack when the opponent is in line (arm extended and point threatening a valid surface) without deflecting the opposing blade;*

(b) if he attempts to find the blade and fails (because of a derobement or trompement) and still continues the attack;

(c) if, in a composite attack, in the course of which his opponent finds the blade, he continues the attack while his opponent immediately ripostes;

(d) if, in a composite attack, he hesitates for a moment during which the opponent delivers a stop thrust, yet he continues his attack;

(e) if, in a composite attack, he is hit by a stop made with the advantage or a period of fencing time before his conclusion;

(f) if he touches by remise, redoublement, or reprise, after a parry by his opponent which is followed by an immediate simple riposte executed in one period of fencing time and without withdrawal of the arm.

3. The fencers are replaced on guard, every time that the Director cannot decide clearly which side is at fault in a double touch.

One of the most difficult cases to decide occurs when there is a stop and there is doubt as to whether it had a sufficient time advantage over the conclusion of a composite attack. In general, in this case, the double touch is the result of simultaneous faults by the fencers, which fact justifies the replacement on guard. (The fault of the attacker lies in indecision, slowness or inefficient feints; the fault of the fencer attacked lies in his delay or slowness in making the stop).

---

*Directors must be alert that the mere grazing of the blades is not considered as sufficient to deflect the opponent's blade.

Electric Foil

Because it is difficult for judges to see touches, electrical touch scoring apparatus has been developed and is now used in all amateur and collegiate fencing competitions. This apparatus replaces the four judges but not the director. The fencing rules are essentially the same when the electric foil is used as they are when the conventional foil is used. Since the fencers are wired to the apparatus, they do not change sides during the bout.

The fencer wears a metallic cloth vest over his regular fencing jacket. The electric foil has a push-button tip and is wired through a groove in the blade. The fencer connects his foil to a body cord which he wears under his jacket and his cord in turn is connected to the scoring device through a reel which takes up slack wire behind the fencer as he retreats.

When a fencer scores a valid touch on the opponent's metallic cloth jacket, a colored light indicates the touch and a buzzer sounds. If he touches off the target, the buzzer sounds and a white light goes on. The bout director must watch both the action and the scoring apparatus lights, and he calls a halt when any light comes on. Now, instead of polling the judges, he observes the lights, determines the right of way, and awards a touch according to his judgment.

It takes only a short time to become accustomed to fencing with the electric foil equipment. The reel wire attached to the back of the fencer offers a slight pull but does not restrict movement. The plastic-lined metallic vest (lame) does retain heat, and the fencer might wish to unzip the vest between bouts. The foil is a bit heavier than a standard foil, especially at the tip, and some practice will be needed to learn to control it.

Most important competitions are fenced on copper mats which are grounded so as to eliminate the problems created by foil tips that touch the floor. On an ungrounded strip, such a touch records as a white light which causes the bout to be halted and denies a fencer the chance to score a touch which might otherwise count.

Tournaments

The most common type of tournament is the round robin in which each contestant meets each of the other fencers in his pool. The person winning the most bouts is declared the winner of the meet. Where the number of entries is large, the meet may be broken up into two or more preliminary pools, followed perhaps by a quarter-final, semi-final, and final rounds. For example, in an intramural meet with 23 entrants, there might be three preliminary pools of six fencers and one of five. The top three places in each pool advances into two semi-final pools of six fencers each. The final round would include the best three from each semi-final.

Another type of tournament is the direct elimination type in which a fencer drops out of the tournament when he is defeated. Occasionally, a meet can be a combination of round robin preliminary pools and a final direct elimination pool.

Figure 22 shows a sample score sheet for a match involving five contestants. Each person fences four bouts and there are ten bouts in the meet.

Name	#	1	2	3	4	5	Won	TS-TR	PL.
Jones	1		$\frac{II}{V}$	$\frac{III}{V}$	$\frac{++++}{D}$	$\frac{++++}{D}$	2	12-15	3RD
Smith	2	$\frac{++++}{D}$		$\frac{0}{V}$	$\frac{++++}{D}$	$\frac{I}{V}$	2	15-11	2ND
White	3	$\frac{++++}{D}$	$\frac{++++}{D}$		$\frac{++++}{D}$	$\frac{III}{V}$	1	9-18	
Baker	4	$\frac{0}{V}$	$\frac{III}{V}$	$\frac{I}{V}$		$\frac{IIII}{V}$	4		1ST
Allen	5	$\frac{II}{V}$	$\frac{++++}{D}$	$\frac{++++}{D}$	$\frac{++++}{D}$		1	13-17	

V = Victory
D = Defeat

Order of bouts:

for pool of 4	pool of 5	pool of 6	
1-4	1-2	1-2	1-4
2-3	3-4	4-5	5-3
1-3	5-1	2-3	1-6
2-4	2-3	5-6	4-2
3-4	5-4	3-1	3-6
1-2	1-3	6-4	5-1
	2-5	2-5	3-4
	4-1		6-2
	3-5		
	4-2		

Figure 22. Round robin score sheet.

In the bout shown scored on the sample score sheet, Jones, #1, lost to Baker, #4, by a score of 5-0. Each time Jones was hit, a tally was marked in column number 4 along line number 1. Baker was not hit, so a zero was marked in column 1 along line 4. Should there be a tie for first place, there will have to be a fence-off. If there is a tie for any place other than first, the tie may be broken by subtracting the total number of touches received (TR) by the fencer from the number of touches that he scored (TS) in that pool. This TS-TR indicator may be a positive or a negative number, and the fencer with the highest indicator has the highest rank in resolving the tie.

Intercollegiate Meets

Men's intercollegiate meets consist of a total of twenty-seven bouts, nine each in foil, epee, and sabre. A college team has nine men with three fencing in each of the three weapons. Each man competes against each of the three opponents in his weapon. The team winning the majority of the bouts, fourteen or more, wins the meet.

The bout order used in college meets requires that one team of three, usually the visitors, fences in a regular rotation while the home team follows a staggered order.

	Visitors		*Home*
Fencer	#1		#1
	#2		#2
	#3		#3
	#1		#2
	#2	vs.	#3
	#3		#1
	#1		#3
	#2		#1
	#3		#2

Where space and equipment is limited, a meet may be fenced on one strip and requires about three hours to run. The trend has been to fencing a dual meet on three strips simultaneously, one weapon match to a strip. A meet of this type can be completed in one hour, but it does require two electrical scoring apparatuses and three directors. The intercollegiate rules are based on the amateur rules and are included in the U.S.F.A. rules book.

This is a period of rapid growth for women's intercollegiate fencing, and meet rules will undoubtedly undergo some changes in the next few years. Some schools are fielding integrated teams with women's foil being a fourth event on coed teams. Where the men's and women's teams are separate, a women's team is made up of four foil fencers each of whom fences against each of the opposing team's fencers. A total of sixteen bouts are fought, and the team with the most victories wins the meet. Where the final score is 8-8, the tie is resolved by counting the total touches scored against the fencers on each team, the team having the fewest being the winner.

STUDY QUESTIONS FOR CHAPTER 5

1. What name is given to the official in charge of the jury?
2. How long is a fencing strip?
3. What are the four votes that may be cast by the jury?
4. If one judge votes "Yes," the other votes "Off-target," and the director votes "No," what must the decision be?
5. What is the difference between validity and materiality?
6. How many officials are needed in an electric foil bout?
7. What does a timekeeper do when there is one minute left?
8. Describe the foil target.
9. What is the penalty for going off the side of the strip with both feet?
10. In Figure 22, White and Allen are tied with one victory apiece. Based on the TS-TR formula, which fencer is in fourth place?
11. In a pool of six fencers, how many bouts will each person fence?
12. Both fencers attack simultaneously and one hits on target while the other touches off-target. What is the director's decision?

chapter 6
A Brief History of Fencing

As one of the major implements of war, the sword was a vital arm for soldiers until the use of firearms became widespread. The ancient Greek, Roman, and Persian soldiers are known to have used swords in battle. Early swordplay was not and did not have to be very artful. The main objective in a fight was to penetrate the opponent's armor, and the accomplishment of this objective required brute strength and a heavy sword rather than finesse and skillful footwork.

Armor became heavier (50 to 70 pounds) and costlier. It was worn in battle by knights on horseback, but as the weapons available to foot soldiers improved, the heavy armor lost its effectiveness (especially if a knight became unhorsed). The best swordsmen turned out to be the foot soldiers who could not afford armor and had to rely on their fencing skills to survive.

The refinement of firearms hastened the end of the use of armor and therefore of the need for heavy swords. Weapons became lighter, but except for the cavalry sabre and the naval cutlas, swords rapidly declined in value as a weapon of war. They were still of use for personal combat, and short, light court swords were worn as a sidearm and also as a matter of fashion. In the field, the bayonet replaced the sword, and early bayonet techniques were essentially the same as those of fencing.

Even in times of peace, the sword played an important role in history. Matters of honor and personal disputes were often settled with the sword, sometimes in impromptu brawls and other times in formal duels for which elaborate codes had been worked out to govern such combat. Since noblemen were more concerned with honor than were men of lower class, they naturally fought the majority of duels (although there is evidence of women having dueled too). The resulting death rates among the nobility rose to such alarming proportions that duels were banned by royal edicts. However, dueling persisted illegally with pistols gaining favor over swords by mid-eighteenth century.

The first fencing schools were opened in Europe in the fifteenth century and at about the same time, the first books on fencing techniques were published.

The lunge, an essential movement in modern fencing, was first suggested about 1575 by a fencing master in Italy. Until that time, the attack had been made by crossing the rear foot in front of the leading foot in what was called a pass. The use of the pass continued through the seventeenth century when it was replaced by the lunge.

A major change in fencing techniques was brought about by the wide use of the rapier in the sixteenth century. The slim-bladed rapier was developed because the use of firearms had made armor ineffective and, hence, heavy swords were no longer needed. The thrust with the point began to replace the cut with the edge of the sword because it came to be realized that a thrust was both quicker and more deadly than a cut.

The swordsmen of the sixteenth and seventeenth centuries found that the rapier was too long and clumsy to be effective for both offense and defense. Therefore, the left hand was used to hold either a dagger, a small shield, a cloak, or even another rapier for defense.

Technique in the use of the sword began to develop rapidly as the light sword made possible many maneuvers that were not practical with rapiers. To prevent eye injuries in practice fencing, it became necessary to control the fast swordplay. Conventions were developed to designate the sequence in which actions could be made.

The invention of the mask by a French fencing master in the late eighteenth century helped to bring about modern fencing. As a result of the use of fencing masks, the old conventions were modified to permit more freedom and speed in fencing actions; consequently, fencing skills became highly developed. As dueling was almost universally illegal by the advent of the nineteenth century, fencing has been practiced primarily as a sport since that time.

The fencing positions in use in the late eighteenth century were pretty much as we know them today. The foil was used first as a training weapon for the dueling sword but soon came into its own as a sporting weapon. The modern epee developed from the rapier and the modern sabre from the cavalry sabre. The present target areas of both were derived from the areas most vulnerable in combat with these weapons.

Since the invention of the mask, the next really major development was the electrical epee which came into world wide use in 1936. Nearly twenty years later, the electrical foil was in use, and now work being completed on developing an electrical sabre.

As weapons became lighter and as less emphasis was put on a fencer's form, mobility increased, and since the first quarter of this century the fencing strip has gradually been increased in length from eighteen feet to the present forty six feet.

Fencing in the United States

Europe has had a long tradition of swordplay, but in the United States the pistol was favored over the sword, and fencing did not find a following until the late nineteenth century. The Amateur Athletic Union conducted a few championships up to 1890, but in 1891 the Amateur Fencers League of America was formed and took over responsibility for developing amateur fencing. In 1981, the A.F.L.A. changed its name to the United States Fencing Association.

In 1884 the Intercollegiate Fencing Association was organized by Columbia, Yale, and Harvard, and today the I.F.A. has thirteen member schools which include some of the strongest teams in the country.

The first national championship for male college fencers was held in 1941 at The Ohio State University. That meet was sponsored by the National Collegiate Athletic Association (N.C.A.A.) and attracted nineteen schools. In recent years, entries have risen to an average of fifty colleges and universities.

The Intercollegiate Women's Fencing Association was founded in 1929 by four eastern schools. In 1971, the association changed its name to the National Intercollegiate Women's Fencing Association and began conducting national championships for college women until 1981 when the Association for Intercollegiate Athletics for Women (A.I.A.W.) took over this responsibility. Some confusion was created in 1982 when both the A.I.A.W. and the N.C.A.A. sponsored women's intercollegiate national championships.

World Fencing

Fencing is one of only six sports to be continuously on the Olympic program since the modern games began in 1896. At this time, European nations dominate the sport as they have throughout fencing history. The leading powers include Russia, Hungary, France, Italy, and Poland.

chapter 7
Class Organization and Teaching Ideas

Suggested Progressions

Course lengths may vary from four to sixteen weeks in length or from eight to thirty class meetings. Class periods may last from twenty-five minutes to a full hour. Since there are so many possible combinations, only a few will be used here in outlining some possible progressions of skills. In every case, however, as much actual fencing time as possible must be arranged.

Assuming an average class period to be forty-five minutes, if eight periods are to be devoted to fencing, include the following skills:

> 6 through 12
> 14, and 18 through 23.

When twelve periods are available, add to the above:

> 24 and 25, and Chapter 4 and 5.

When sixteen class periods are possible, include skills:

> 1 through 28, and Chapters 4 and 5.

For courses that include more periods than the above, follow the text sequentially from skill 1 as far on as time allows. But regardless of the length of the course, some bouting should be permitted each day after skill 22 has been covered. By skill 28, an occasional full period can be devoted to bouting, particularly if Chapters 4 and 5 have been assigned.

Considerations in Course Planning

When first confronted with the problem of planning a unit or course in fencing, the new teacher is likely to think merely in terms of establishing a skill sequence and may overlook many important considerations. Each teaching situation is sufficiently different as to require unique planning.

The teacher's objectives will be quite different when preparing a recreation course for adults as compared to a high school physical education fencing unit. We might identify four types of instructional settings:

1. The nonschool setting in which the role of the teacher is to impart fencing skills to students, perhaps varying widely in ages and abilities, who have paid some private agency for the course. Most of these students will not fence again when the course is completed and probably took the course for some recreation or exercise. In this category are classes sponsored by a Y.M.C.A., Y.W.C.A., a J.C.C., or an adult education program of a city.

2. The nonschool setting of a fencing club or salle d'armes which employs a well-qualified instructor or fencing master (maitre d'armes) normally provides continuing instruction to both recreational and competitive fencers. The club may employ the teacher part- or full-time, or the club may be owned and operated by the teacher.

3. The high school or college setting where a physical education teacher gives instruction in fencing. He is generally not a specialist in fencing and teaches many other sports skills. Unlike the first two settings that have been discussed, this is an educational setting where grading must be done and some concomitant outcomes are often sought such as sportsmanship, cooperation with others, and care of the body. Another difference is that often the pupils do not take the course voluntarily and do not pay the instructor. For most students, it is a terminal experience, but others will join a club or team or will enter an intramural tournament.

4. The fencing team setting in a school or college where a coach develops a competitive team. Here the activity is not only elective on the part of the student but selective on the part of the coach. The coach may recruit team members from high schools that have fencing or he may provide instruction to beginners. He may or may not be part of the school faculty; he may be part-time or full-time; and he may be an amateur or a professional. Whatever his status, his role is broader than teachers in the other three settings in that he must recruit, administer a budget, schedule meets, order and repair equipment, and develop a balanced, winning team.

The quality of fencing teachers in the various situations ranges from barely adequate to excellent. The less confident teachers cannot and should not try to handle large classes, and, for any teacher, ideal class sizes depend upon the availability of equipment and space, the motivation of the students, and even on the expected levels of noise from adjacent activities. Classes of up to twenty pupils are manageable. An assistant or two may be needed for larger classes, depending on the age and abilities of the students.

In course planning, a number of questions must be answered if the teacher is to intelligently plan his lessons:

1. Is the course terminal or will most of the students continue to the next level? Where the pupils are expected to take further instruction, more time may be spent on teaching correct fundamentals. Where the students will have no further fencing experiences, the course can focus on the specific short-term needs of the class.

2. What are the motives of the students for taking fencing? If the course is required, the instructor can expect some resistance to learning, whereas an elective course is easier to teach since the students chose the activity. Students often take an activity to meet specific needs such as getting exercise, increasing flexibility, improving posture, preparing to try out for the team, or, in the case of theatre majors, learning a skill vital to their professional background.

3. What is the age level, sex, and physical condition of the students? A class of twelve year olds will not be taught in the same manner as will a class of middle-aged men. A coed class should be handled slightly differently from a segregated one.

4. Will the facilities and equipment be adequate for the number of students in the class? Advanced notice of the expected problems will allow some time to work out the necessary adjustments.

5. How many meetings will there be and what is the length of each period? The teacher must plan which skills he can teach in the allotted time, the sequence in which he will teach them, and how thoroughly he can teach them. Keeping in mind the objectives for the particular course, the teacher should establish the competencies he expects by the end of the course and should then proceed to plan backwards, period by period, the skills he will be able to include to achieve the desired outcomes.

6. Will grades have to be given? If so, the teacher must plan time for evaluation and must decide whether a written examination will be given. Evaluation is a most difficult task because the only real criterion is whether or not the student can win. Good form can be expected, of course, and the student may be asked

to demonstrate his ability to perform various offensive and defensive skills. But too often these are tested in a nonbout setting, and even then the evaluation is subjective. The student's showing against any given partner is largely dependent on the quality of that partner, and he will perform somewhat differently against different partners. This is not to say that evaluation is impossible. But, for an inexperienced teacher, grading in fencing is much more difficult than in a sport where there are some objective measures such as time, distance, or accuracy.

7. What are the limitations of the teacher? This final question is an important one in course planning. The teacher must make an honest appraisal of his competence so that he does not undertake the teaching of a course that is beyond his ability. There is, after all, an element of danger and therefore a concern for liability that has to be considered. However, given even modest fencing skills, the average physical education teacher can do a respectable job of instructing beginning fencing, particularly if he seeks occasional advice from others with experience and reads books on fencing.

Learning Patterns of Beginners

A typical class will include pupils with a wide range of physical skills and mental abilities. The very first day will reveal students who are quick, enthusiastic, coordinated, and attentive. Unfortunately, some will be slow, lethargic, inattentive, and uncoordinated, but most will be between these extremes. Good instruction usually has the effect of widening the differences between the best and the weakest pupils, because the well-coordinated students learn more rapidly. As the gap widens, the teacher may need to group his class according to ability.

At first the class as a whole will make very rapid progress because the early skills involve the large locomotor muscles. As control of the body and legs increases, the learning emphasis is shifted to the use of the blade. This is the stage where coordination differences become really evident because the smaller muscles of the forearm, hand, and fingers must exercise finer control of movement.

Next, individual styles start to emerge, and whatever seems to work for each student is reinforced, while that which does not work is neglected or discarded. A point is reached where some students have formed correct habits and continue to develop while others reach a plateau because of the limitations imposed by some incorrect habits.

Once a student has achieved control of both his body and his blade, his mind is then free for analysis and tactical thought. It is at this level when real appreciation and enjoyment of the sport are possible.

Organization and Methods

There are a few common formations and methods for grouping the students. Each has its value for specific stages.

1.   Single line: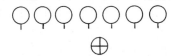

This is a good formation for initial instruction in footwork and lunging. Left-handers should be to the instructor's right.

2.   Double line of paired partners:

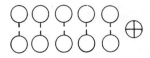

This is the most common and useful formation. It permits easy rotation of partners.

3.   Circle of paired partners:

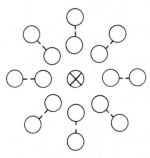

This has the advantage of centrally locating the instructor when a new blade skill is being taught. He is within a few steps of everyone.

4.   Ability groupings: The students may or may not be physically isolated in their groups and any of the above formations may be utilized. Grouping is most justified when the class is large, when teaching assistance is available, when the course lasts a full quarter or semester, or when new students are added to the class from time to time. The obvious advantages are that the best

students can move ahead rapidly, the weakest students are not forced to keep pace with the whole class, and new students or students who have missed classes have an opportunity to catch up.

5.   Individual lessons: Where clases are small or when preparing students for competition, individual instruction is necessary. The instructor can gear each lesson to the needs of the individual and can act the role of an opponent as well as of a teacher. It is the most effective type of instruction but the least efficient for classes.

Since most class work is done in the double line formation, it will save the instructor a great deal of time if he teaches the partners to work together as teacher-pupils. As the instructor moves about the class, he should point out each student's errors not only to the student but to his partner as well, and the partner should be urged to watch for particular errors. Thus, at any given time, half of the students are playing a teacher role.

When teaching a coed class, remember that women need added protection in the chest. It is not necessary to pair women with women and men with men, although at times that seems to work best. But if a tall, strong boy is paired with a much smaller girl, the boy must be advised to exercise some control over the power of his lunges. Generally, no adjustments are necessary when boys and girls of average height are paired.

Evaluation

Skill testing can be a continuous process or one that is reserved for the end of the course. There are a number of useful ways to evaluate students. For a large class, a simple method is to select only a few representative skills and test two students at a time while the rest of the class practices.

While some weight can be given to a student's bouting ability, it is unwise to give a grade based entirely on bout results because very often an aggressive, athletic student will defeat others who may well have better skills and form. Also, student judges cannot give accurate and consistent calls on touches.

There are no completely useful, standardized skills or written tests for fencing. Teachers will develop their own tests based on the material they have covered and the book that was used.

Teaching Tips

It is especially helpful if, before the first class meeting, you mark all of the foils in a manner that will make it easy for a student to locate the top surface of his foil handle. This can be accomplished by putting a smudge of ink with a marking pen on the top surface of the blade just in front of the bell. Left-handed foils should be marked distinctly, possibly by placing a piece of tape on the bell.

Masks should be marked with a number and a size so that students can easily locate and use the same masks each period.

A common teaching method is to explain the skill, demonstrate it, allow the class to practice for a time, demonstrate again, and again allow for practice. The process can be made more effective if the students are required to read material on the skill before coming to class.

The teacher may need to give verbal commands at first, and some teachers are more comfortable working "by the numbers," but such drills are artificial and restrictive.

Some common errors in teaching that must be avoided are:

1. Holding a class in one position while the teacher makes individual corrections. Boredom and fatigue will result.
2. Overworking a class early in the course before reasonable condition has been acquired. Give frequent rest breaks.
3. Allowing too much fencing too early. This can only lead to the formation of poor habits and broken blades.
4. Teaching too many skills in one period. This can overwhelm the students with the consequence that nothing is learned well.
5. Including every foil skill in a relatively short course. Some inexperienced instructors are not sure what is important and what can be excluded and so cram everything in just to be on the safe side. Actually, for a short fencing unit, only a few skills are essential and, if the teaching effort is concentrated on these, the students can find considerable enjoyment in fencing.

In summary, fencing is a difficult sport to teach, but, with some study and thought, a teacher with a little training in fencing can handle a beginning class.

SELECTED REFERENCES

Alaux, Michel. *Modern Fencing.* New York: Charles Scribner's Sons, 1975.

Anderson, Bob. *All About Fencing.* London: Stanley Paul and Co., 1970.

Bower, Muriel. *Fencing.* Dubuque: Wm. C. Brown Company Publishers, 1980.

Castello, Julio M. *The Theory and Practice of Fencing.* New York: Charles Scribner's Sons, 1933.

Deladrier, Clovis. *Modern Fencing.* Annapolis: United States Naval Institute, 1948.

Gillet, Jean-Jacques. *Foil Techniques and Terminology.* Livingston, N.J.: United States Academy of Arms, 1981.

Lukovich, Istvan. *Electric Foil Fencing.* Budapest: Corvina Press, 1971.

N.A.G.W.S. Rules. *Archery-Fencing May 1980-1982.* American Alliance for Health, Physical Education, Recreation, and Dance, 1980.

Palffy-Alpar, Julius. *Sword and Masque.* Philadelphia: F.A. Davis Co., 1967.

United States Fencing Association. *Fencing Rules.* Authorized translation of F.I.E. rules published by U.S.F.A., 601 Curtis St., Albany, CA. 94706, 1982.

INDEX

Advance, 13, 21-22
Advance lunge, 42
A.I.A.W., 83
Amateur Fencers League of
    America, 2, 83
Attention, 11, 18

Ballestra, 43
Beat attack, 37, 45-47, 53
Beat and disengagement, 47
Bind, 59
Boundaries, 67-68, 83
Bouts, 36, 61
Breaking the line, 56

Change of engagement, 30
Closing the line, 30-32
Corps-a-corps, 73
Counter parries, 43-44
Cutover, 54, 74

Defense, varieties of, 56
Director, 24, 69, 71, 72, 74, 75
Disarming, 17
Disengagement, 37-38, 50, 54
Disengage riposte, 52
Double, 44-45, 47, 48
Double touch, 72, 75
Doubtful touch, 72, 73

Electric foil, 69, 76
Engagement, 28, 29
    change of, 30
Epee, 3, 4, 5, 82
Equipment, 7
Etiquette, 65
Evaluation, 90

False attack, 41, 46, 54, 56
Feints, 37, 38, 39, 40, 45, 48
Flèche, 57-58
Foils, 4, 7, 17, 46

Glide, 59
Gloves, 9
Grip, 17, 18

History, 81-83
Hit, 26

Indicators, 78
Infighting, 73
Intercollegiate meets, 78, 83
Invitation, 55-56, 59

Jackets, 8
Judging, 69-70, 72, 74
Jury, 69

Line closing, 30-32
Low line,
    attacks, 48
    parries, 48-50
Lunge, 14-15, 23-24, 26-28

Maitre d'armes, 2, 86
Masks, 8, 25
Materiality of touch, 69, 72

N.C.A.A., 2, 3, 83
N.I.W.F.A., 3, 83

On-guard, 12, 20-21
One-two, 39-40, 47
One-two-three, 39

Parries,
   one, 50-51
   two, 51
   three, 51
   four, 32, 47
   five, 51
   six, 33, 47
   seven, 48-49
   eight, 49-50
Penalties, 5, 68
Phrase, 61, 69, 73, 74
Point in line, 37, 53-54, 59, 74
Positions of blade, 34, 55
Pressure, 58

Recovery from lunge, 5, 14, 15, 23
Redoublement, 51-52, 75
Remise, 52, 75
Retreat, 13, 22
Right of way, 36, 37, 45, 46, 53,
   69, 74
Riposte, 26, 34-36, 37, 44, 50

Sabre, 3, 4, 5, 69, 70, 73
Safety, 16
Salute, 18-19
Scorekeeper, 70-71
Scoring, 68, 77
Scoring machine operator, 71
Stop hit, 53, 54, 74, 75

Tactics, 54, 61-65
Target area, 67
Timekeeper, 71
Time limits, 69
Tournaments, 76-77

United States Fencing Association,
   3, 69, 78, 83
United States Fencing Coaches
   Association, 2

Validity of touch, 69
Votes, 71-72
Voting table, 73